Mometrix TEST PREPARATION

Virginia

SOL World History and Geography to 1500 A.D. Secrets Study Guide

Dear Future Exam Success Story

First of all, **THANK YOU** for purchasing Mometrix study materials!

Second, congratulations! You are one of the few determined test-takers who are committed to doing whatever it takes to excel on your exam. **You have come to the right place.** We developed these study materials with one goal in mind: to deliver you the information you need in a format that's concise and easy to use.

In addition to optimizing your guide for the content of the test, we've outlined our recommended steps for breaking down the preparation process into small, attainable goals so you can make sure you stay on track.

We've also analyzed the entire test-taking process, identifying the most common pitfalls and showing how you can overcome them and be ready for any curveball the test throws you.

Standardized testing is one of the biggest obstacles on your road to success, which only increases the importance of doing well in the high-pressure, high-stakes environment of test day. Your results on this test could have a significant impact on your future, and this guide provides the information and practical advice to help you achieve your full potential on test day.

Your success is our success

We would love to hear from you! If you would like to share the story of your exam success or if you have any questions or comments in regard to our products, please contact us at **800-673-8175** or **support@mometrix.com**.

Thanks again for your business and we wish you continued success!

Sincerely,
The Mometrix Test Preparation Team

Need more help? Check out our flashcards at:
http://MometrixFlashcards.com/SOL

Written and edited by the Mometrix Exam Secrets Test Prep Team
Printed in the United States of America

TABLE OF CONTENTS

Introduction

Thank you for purchasing this resource! You have made the choice to prepare yourself for a test that could have a huge impact on your future, and this guide is designed to help you be fully ready for test day. Obviously, it's important to have a solid understanding of the test material, but you also need to be prepared for the unique environment and stressors of the test, so that you can perform to the best of your abilities.

For this purpose, the first section that appears in this guide is the **Secret Keys**. We've devoted countless hours to meticulously researching what works and what doesn't, and we've boiled down our findings to the five most impactful steps you can take to improve your performance on the test. We start at the beginning with study planning and move through the preparation process, all the way to the testing strategies that will help you get the most out of what you know when you're finally sitting in front of the test.

We recommend that you start preparing for your test as far in advance as possible. However, if you've bought this guide as a last-minute study resource and only have a few days before your test, we recommend that you skip over the first two Secret Keys since they address a long-term study plan.

If you struggle with **test anxiety**, we strongly encourage you to check out our recommendations for how you can overcome it. Test anxiety is a formidable foe, but it can be beaten, and we want to make sure you have the tools you need to defeat it.

Secret Key #1 – Plan Big, Study Small

There's a lot riding on your performance. If you want to ace this test, you're going to need to keep your skills sharp and the material fresh in your mind. You need a plan that lets you review everything you need to know while still fitting in your schedule. We'll break this strategy down into three categories.

Information Organization

Start with the information you already have: the official test outline. From this, you can make a complete list of all the concepts you need to cover before the test. Organize these concepts into groups that can be studied together, and create a list of any related vocabulary you need to learn so you can brush up on any difficult terms. You'll want to keep this vocabulary list handy once you actually start studying since you may need to add to it along the way.

Time Management

Once you have your set of study concepts, decide how to spread them out over the time you have left before the test. Break your study plan into small, clear goals so you have a manageable task for each day and know exactly what you're doing. Then just focus on one small step at a time. When you manage your time this way, you don't need to spend hours at a time studying. Studying a small block of content for a short period each day helps you retain information better and avoid stressing over how much you have left to do. You can relax knowing that you have a plan to cover everything in time. In order for this strategy to be effective though, you have to start studying early and stick to your schedule. Avoid the exhaustion and futility that comes from last-minute cramming!

Study Environment

The environment you study in has a big impact on your learning. Studying in a coffee shop, while probably more enjoyable, is not likely to be as fruitful as studying in a quiet room. It's important to keep distractions to a minimum. You're only planning to study for a short block of time, so make the most of it. Don't pause to check your phone or get up to find a snack. It's also important to **avoid multitasking**. Research has consistently shown that multitasking will make your studying dramatically less effective. Your study area should also be comfortable and well-lit so you don't have the distraction of straining your eyes or sitting on an uncomfortable chair.

The time of day you study is also important. You want to be rested and alert. Don't wait until just before bedtime. Study when you'll be most likely to comprehend and remember. Even better, if you know what time of day your test will be, set that time aside for study. That way your brain will be used to working on that subject at that specific time and you'll have a better chance of recalling information.

Finally, it can be helpful to team up with others who are studying for the same test. Your actual studying should be done in as isolated an environment as possible, but the work of organizing the information and setting up the study plan can be divided up. In between study sessions, you can discuss with your teammates the concepts that you're all studying and quiz each other on the details. Just be sure that your teammates are as serious about the test as you are. If you find that your study time is being replaced with social time, you might need to find a new team.

Secret Key #2 – Make Your Studying Count

You're devoting a lot of time and effort to preparing for this test, so you want to be absolutely certain it will pay off. This means doing more than just reading the content and hoping you can remember it on test day. It's important to make every minute of study count. There are two main areas you can focus on to make your studying count.

Retention

It doesn't matter how much time you study if you can't remember the material. You need to make sure you are retaining the concepts. To check your retention of the information you're learning, try recalling it at later times with minimal prompting. Try carrying around flashcards and glance at one or two from time to time or ask a friend who's also studying for the test to quiz you.

To enhance your retention, look for ways to put the information into practice so that you can apply it rather than simply recalling it. If you're using the information in practical ways, it will be much easier to remember. Similarly, it helps to solidify a concept in your mind if you're not only reading it to yourself but also explaining it to someone else. Ask a friend to let you teach them about a concept you're a little shaky on (or speak aloud to an imaginary audience if necessary). As you try to summarize, define, give examples, and answer your friend's questions, you'll understand the concepts better and they will stay with you longer. Finally, step back for a big picture view and ask yourself how each piece of information fits with the whole subject. When you link the different concepts together and see them working together as a whole, it's easier to remember the individual components.

Finally, practice showing your work on any multi-step problems, even if you're just studying. Writing out each step you take to solve a problem will help solidify the process in your mind, and you'll be more likely to remember it during the test.

Modality

Modality simply refers to the means or method by which you study. Choosing a study modality that fits your own individual learning style is crucial. No two people learn best in exactly the same way, so it's important to know your strengths and use them to your advantage.

For example, if you learn best by visualization, focus on visualizing a concept in your mind and draw an image or a diagram. Try color-coding your notes, illustrating them, or creating symbols that will trigger your mind to recall a learned concept. If you learn best by hearing or discussing information, find a study partner who learns the same way or read aloud to yourself. Think about how to put the information in your own words. Imagine that you are giving a lecture on the topic and record yourself so you can listen to it later.

For any learning style, flashcards can be helpful. Organize the information so you can take advantage of spare moments to review. Underline key words or phrases. Use different colors for different categories. Mnemonic devices (such as creating a short list in which every item starts with the same letter) can also help with retention. Find what works best for you and use it to store the information in your mind most effectively and easily.

Secret Key #3 – Practice the Right Way

Your success on test day depends not only on how many hours you put into preparing, but also on whether you prepared the right way. It's good to check along the way to see if your studying is paying off. One of the most effective ways to do this is by taking practice tests to evaluate your progress. Practice tests are useful because they show exactly where you need to improve. Every time you take a practice test, pay special attention to these three groups of questions:

- The questions you got wrong
- The questions you had to guess on, even if you guessed right
- The questions you found difficult or slow to work through

This will show you exactly what your weak areas are, and where you need to devote more study time. Ask yourself why each of these questions gave you trouble. Was it because you didn't understand the material? Was it because you didn't remember the vocabulary? Do you need more repetitions on this type of question to build speed and confidence? Dig into those questions and figure out how you can strengthen your weak areas as you go back to review the material.

Additionally, many practice tests have a section explaining the answer choices. It can be tempting to read the explanation and think that you now have a good understanding of the concept. However, an explanation likely only covers part of the question's broader context. Even if the explanation makes perfect sense, **go back and investigate** every concept related to the question until you're positive you have a thorough understanding.

As you go along, keep in mind that the practice test is just that: practice. Memorizing these questions and answers will not be very helpful on the actual test because it is unlikely to have any of the same exact questions. If you only know the right answers to the sample questions, you won't be prepared for the real thing. **Study the concepts** until you understand them fully, and then you'll be able to answer any question that shows up on the test.

It's important to wait on the practice tests until you're ready. If you take a test on your first day of study, you may be overwhelmed by the amount of material covered and how much you need to learn. Work up to it gradually.

On test day, you'll need to be prepared for answering questions, managing your time, and using the test-taking strategies you've learned. It's a lot to balance, like a mental marathon that will have a big impact on your future. Like training for a marathon, you'll need to start slowly and work your way up. When test day arrives, you'll be ready.

Start with the strategies you've read in the first two Secret Keys—plan your course and study in the way that works best for you. If you have time, consider using multiple study resources to get different approaches to the same concepts. It can be helpful to see difficult concepts from more than one angle. Then find a good source for practice tests. Many times, the test website will suggest potential study resources or provide sample tests.

Practice Test Strategy

If you're able to find at least three practice tests, we recommend this strategy:

Untimed and Open-Book Practice

Take the first test with no time constraints and with your notes and study guide handy. Take your time and focus on applying the strategies you've learned.

Timed and Open-Book Practice

Take the second practice test open-book as well, but set a timer and practice pacing yourself to finish in time.

Timed and Closed-Book Practice

Take any other practice tests as if it were test day. Set a timer and put away your study materials. Sit at a table or desk in a quiet room, imagine yourself at the testing center, and answer questions as quickly and accurately as possible.

Keep repeating timed and closed-book tests on a regular basis until you run out of practice tests or it's time for the actual test. Your mind will be ready for the schedule and stress of test day, and you'll be able to focus on recalling the material you've learned.

Secret Key #4 – Pace Yourself

Once you're fully prepared for the material on the test, your biggest challenge on test day will be managing your time. Just knowing that the clock is ticking can make you panic even if you have plenty of time left. Work on pacing yourself so you can build confidence against the time constraints of the exam. Pacing is a difficult skill to master, especially in a high-pressure environment, so **practice is vital**.

Set time expectations for your pace based on how much time is available. For example, if a section has 60 questions and the time limit is 30 minutes, you know you have to average 30 seconds or less per question in order to answer them all. Although 30 seconds is the hard limit, set 25 seconds per question as your goal, so you reserve extra time to spend on harder questions. When you budget extra time for the harder questions, you no longer have any reason to stress when those questions take longer to answer.

Don't let this time expectation distract you from working through the test at a calm, steady pace, but keep it in mind so you don't spend too much time on any one question. Recognize that taking extra time on one question you don't understand may keep you from answering two that you do understand later in the test. If your time limit for a question is up and you're still not sure of the answer, mark it and move on, and come back to it later if the time and the test format allow. If the testing format doesn't allow you to return to earlier questions, just make an educated guess; then put it out of your mind and move on.

On the easier questions, be careful not to rush. It may seem wise to hurry through them so you have more time for the challenging ones, but it's not worth missing one if you know the concept and just didn't take the time to read the question fully. Work efficiently but make sure you understand the question and have looked at all of the answer choices, since more than one may seem right at first.

Even if you're paying attention to the time, you may find yourself a little behind at some point. You should speed up to get back on track, but do so wisely. Don't panic; just take a few seconds less on each question until you're caught up. Don't guess without thinking, but do look through the answer choices and eliminate any you know are wrong. If you can get down to two choices, it is often worthwhile to guess from those. Once you've chosen an answer, move on and don't dwell on any that you skipped or had to hurry through. If a question was taking too long, chances are it was one of the harder ones, so you weren't as likely to get it right anyway.

On the other hand, if you find yourself getting ahead of schedule, it may be beneficial to slow down a little. The more quickly you work, the more likely you are to make a careless mistake that will affect your score. You've budgeted time for each question, so don't be afraid to spend that time. Practice an efficient but careful pace to get the most out of the time you have.

Secret Key #5 – Have a Plan for Guessing

When you're taking the test, you may find yourself stuck on a question. Some of the answer choices seem better than others, but you don't see the one answer choice that is obviously correct. What do you do?

The scenario described above is very common, yet most test takers have not effectively prepared for it. Developing and practicing a plan for guessing may be one of the single most effective uses of your time as you get ready for the exam.

In developing your plan for guessing, there are three questions to address:

- When should you start the guessing process?
- How should you narrow down the choices?
- Which answer should you choose?

When to Start the Guessing Process

Unless your plan for guessing is to select C every time (which, despite its merits, is not what we recommend), you need to leave yourself enough time to apply your answer elimination strategies. Since you have a limited amount of time for each question, that means that if you're going to give yourself the best shot at guessing correctly, you have to decide quickly whether or not you will guess.

Of course, the best-case scenario is that you don't have to guess at all, so first, see if you can answer the question based on your knowledge of the subject and basic reasoning skills. Focus on the key words in the question and try to jog your memory of related topics. Give yourself a chance to bring the knowledge to mind, but once you realize that you don't have (or you can't access) the knowledge you need to answer the question, it's time to start the guessing process.

It's almost always better to start the guessing process too early than too late. It only takes a few seconds to remember something and answer the question from knowledge. Carefully eliminating wrong answer choices takes longer. Plus, going through the process of eliminating answer choices can actually help jog your memory.

Summary: Start the guessing process as soon as you decide that you can't answer the question based on your knowledge.

How to Narrow Down the Choices

The next chapter in this book (**Test-Taking Strategies**) includes a wide range of strategies for how to approach questions and how to look for answer choices to eliminate. You will definitely want to read those carefully, practice them, and figure out which ones work best for you. Here though, we're going to address a mindset rather than a particular strategy.

Your odds of guessing an answer correctly depend on how many options you are choosing from.

Number of options left	5	4	3	2	1
Odds of guessing correctly	20%	25%	33%	50%	100%

You can see from this chart just how valuable it is to be able to eliminate incorrect answers and make an educated guess, but there are two things that many test takers do that cause them to miss out on the benefits of guessing:

- Accidentally eliminating the correct answer
- Selecting an answer based on an impression

We'll look at the first one here, and the second one in the next section.

To avoid accidentally eliminating the correct answer, we recommend a thought exercise called **the $5 challenge**. In this challenge, you only eliminate an answer choice from contention if you are willing to bet $5 on it being wrong. Why $5? Five dollars is a small but not insignificant amount of money. It's an amount you could afford to lose but wouldn't want to throw away. And while losing $5 once might not hurt too much, doing it twenty times will set you back $100. In the same way, each small decision you make—eliminating a choice here, guessing on a question there—won't by itself impact your score very much, but when you put them all together, they can make a big difference. By holding each answer choice elimination decision to a higher standard, you can reduce the risk of accidentally eliminating the correct answer.

The $5 challenge can also be applied in a positive sense: If you are willing to bet $5 that an answer choice *is* correct, go ahead and mark it as correct.

Summary: Only eliminate an answer choice if you are willing to bet $5 that it is wrong.

Which Answer to Choose

You're taking the test. You've run into a hard question and decided you'll have to guess. You've eliminated all the answer choices you're willing to bet $5 on. Now you have to pick an answer. Why do we even need to talk about this? Why can't you just pick whichever one you feel like when the time comes?

The answer to these questions is that if you don't come into the test with a plan, you'll rely on your impression to select an answer choice, and if you do that, you risk falling into a trap. The test writers know that everyone who takes their test will be guessing on some of the questions, so they intentionally write wrong answer choices to seem plausible. You still have to pick an answer though, and if the wrong answer choices are designed to look right, how can you ever be sure that you're not falling for their trap? The best solution we've found to this dilemma is to take the decision out of your hands entirely. Here is the process we recommend:

Once you've eliminated any choices that you are confident (willing to bet $5) are wrong, select the first remaining choice as your answer.

Whether you choose to select the first remaining choice, the second, or the last, the important thing is that you use some preselected standard. Using this approach guarantees that you will not be enticed into selecting an answer choice that looks right, because you are not basing your decision on how the answer choices look.

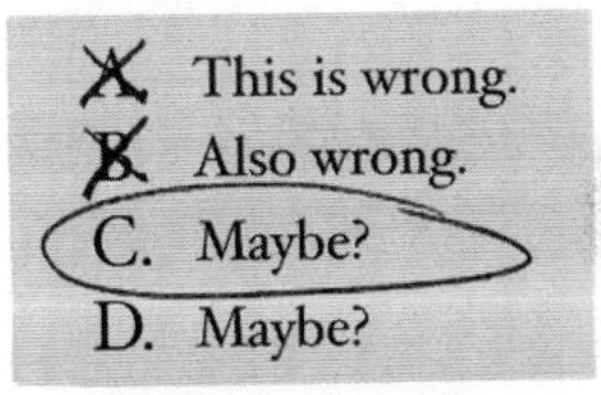

This is not meant to make you question your knowledge. Instead, it is to help you recognize the difference between your knowledge and your impressions. There's a huge difference between thinking an answer is right because of what you know, and thinking an answer is right because it looks or sounds like it should be right.

Summary: To ensure that your selection is appropriately random, make a predetermined selection from among all answer choices you have not eliminated.

Test-Taking Strategies

This section contains a list of test-taking strategies that you may find helpful as you work through the test. By taking what you know and applying logical thought, you can maximize your chances of answering any question correctly!

It is very important to realize that every question is different and every person is different: no single strategy will work on every question, and no single strategy will work for every person. That's why we've included all of them here, so you can try them out and determine which ones work best for different types of questions and which ones work best for you.

Question Strategies

✓ Read Carefully

Read the question and the answer choices carefully. Don't miss the question because you misread the terms. You have plenty of time to read each question thoroughly and make sure you understand what is being asked. Yet a happy medium must be attained, so don't waste too much time. You must read carefully and efficiently.

✓ Contextual Clues

Look for contextual clues. If the question includes a word you are not familiar with, look at the immediate context for some indication of what the word might mean. Contextual clues can often give you all the information you need to decipher the meaning of an unfamiliar word. Even if you can't determine the meaning, you may be able to narrow down the possibilities enough to make a solid guess at the answer to the question.

✓ Prefixes

If you're having trouble with a word in the question or answer choices, try dissecting it. Take advantage of every clue that the word might include. Prefixes can be a huge help. Usually, they allow you to determine a basic meaning. *Pre-* means before, *post-* means after, *pro-* is positive, *de-* is negative. From prefixes, you can get an idea of the general meaning of the word and try to put it into context.

✓ Hedge Words

Watch out for critical hedge words, such as *likely, may, can, often, almost, mostly, usually, generally, rarely,* and *sometimes.* Question writers insert these hedge phrases to cover every possibility. Often an answer choice will be wrong simply because it leaves no room for exception. Be on guard for answer choices that have definitive words such as *exactly* and *always.*

✓ Switchback Words

Stay alert for *switchbacks.* These are the words and phrases frequently used to alert you to shifts in thought. The most common switchback words are *but, although,* and *however.* Others include *nevertheless, on the other hand, even though, while, in spite of, despite,* and *regardless of.* Switchback words are important to catch because they can change the direction of the question or an answer choice.

⊘ FACE VALUE

When in doubt, use common sense. Accept the situation in the problem at face value. Don't read too much into it. These problems will not require you to make wild assumptions. If you have to go beyond creativity and warp time or space in order to have an answer choice fit the question, then you should move on and consider the other answer choices. These are normal problems rooted in reality. The applicable relationship or explanation may not be readily apparent, but it is there for you to figure out. Use your common sense to interpret anything that isn't clear.

Answer Choice Strategies

⊘ ANSWER SELECTION

The most thorough way to pick an answer choice is to identify and eliminate wrong answers until only one is left, then confirm it is the correct answer. Sometimes an answer choice may immediately seem right, but be careful. The test writers will usually put more than one reasonable answer choice on each question, so take a second to read all of them and make sure that the other choices are not equally obvious. As long as you have time left, it is better to read every answer choice than to pick the first one that looks right without checking the others.

⊘ ANSWER CHOICE FAMILIES

An answer choice family consists of two (in rare cases, three) answer choices that are very similar in construction and cannot all be true at the same time. If you see two answer choices that are direct opposites or parallels, one of them is usually the correct answer. For instance, if one answer choice says that quantity x increases and another either says that quantity x decreases (opposite) or says that quantity y increases (parallel), then those answer choices would fall into the same family. An answer choice that doesn't match the construction of the answer choice family is more likely to be incorrect. Most questions will not have answer choice families, but when they do appear, you should be prepared to recognize them.

⊘ ELIMINATE ANSWERS

Eliminate answer choices as soon as you realize they are wrong, but make sure you consider all possibilities. If you are eliminating answer choices and realize that the last one you are left with is also wrong, don't panic. Start over and consider each choice again. There may be something you missed the first time that you will realize on the second pass.

⊘ AVOID FACT TRAPS

Don't be distracted by an answer choice that is factually true but doesn't answer the question. You are looking for the choice that answers the question. Stay focused on what the question is asking for so you don't accidentally pick an answer that is true but incorrect. Always go back to the question and make sure the answer choice you've selected actually answers the question and is not merely a true statement.

⊘ EXTREME STATEMENTS

In general, you should avoid answers that put forth extreme actions as standard practice or proclaim controversial ideas as established fact. An answer choice that states the "process should be used in certain situations, if..." is much more likely to be correct than one that states the "process should be discontinued completely." The first is a calm rational statement and doesn't even make a definitive, uncompromising stance, using a hedge word *if* to provide wiggle room, whereas the second choice is far more extreme.

✓ Benchmark

As you read through the answer choices and you come across one that seems to answer the question well, mentally select that answer choice. This is not your final answer, but it's the one that will help you evaluate the other answer choices. The one that you selected is your benchmark or standard for judging each of the other answer choices. Every other answer choice must be compared to your benchmark. That choice is correct until proven otherwise by another answer choice beating it. If you find a better answer, then that one becomes your new benchmark. Once you've decided that no other choice answers the question as well as your benchmark, you have your final answer.

✓ Predict the Answer

Before you even start looking at the answer choices, it is often best to try to predict the answer. When you come up with the answer on your own, it is easier to avoid distractions and traps because you will know exactly what to look for. The right answer choice is unlikely to be word-for-word what you came up with, but it should be a close match. Even if you are confident that you have the right answer, you should still take the time to read each option before moving on.

General Strategies

✓ Tough Questions

If you are stumped on a problem or it appears too hard or too difficult, don't waste time. Move on! Remember though, if you can quickly check for obviously incorrect answer choices, your chances of guessing correctly are greatly improved. Before you completely give up, at least try to knock out a couple of possible answers. Eliminate what you can and then guess at the remaining answer choices before moving on.

✓ Check Your Work

Since you will probably not know every term listed and the answer to every question, it is important that you get credit for the ones that you do know. Don't miss any questions through careless mistakes. If at all possible, try to take a second to look back over your answer selection and make sure you've selected the correct answer choice and haven't made a costly careless mistake (such as marking an answer choice that you didn't mean to mark). This quick double check should more than pay for itself in caught mistakes for the time it costs.

✓ Pace Yourself

It's easy to be overwhelmed when you're looking at a page full of questions; your mind is confused and full of random thoughts, and the clock is ticking down faster than you would like. Calm down and maintain the pace that you have set for yourself. Especially as you get down to the last few minutes of the test, don't let the small numbers on the clock make you panic. As long as you are on track by monitoring your pace, you are guaranteed to have time for each question.

✓ Don't Rush

It is very easy to make errors when you are in a hurry. Maintaining a fast pace in answering questions is pointless if it makes you miss questions that you would have gotten right otherwise. Test writers like to include distracting information and wrong answers that seem right. Taking a little extra time to avoid careless mistakes can make all the difference in your test score. Find a pace that allows you to be confident in the answers that you select.

☑ KEEP MOVING

Panicking will not help you pass the test, so do your best to stay calm and keep moving. Taking deep breaths and going through the answer elimination steps you practiced can help to break through a stress barrier and keep your pace.

Final Notes

The combination of a solid foundation of content knowledge and the confidence that comes from practicing your plan for applying that knowledge is the key to maximizing your performance on test day. As your foundation of content knowledge is built up and strengthened, you'll find that the strategies included in this chapter become more and more effective in helping you quickly sift through the distractions and traps of the test to isolate the correct answer.

Now that you're preparing to move forward into the test content chapters of this book, be sure to keep your goal in mind. As you read, think about how you will be able to apply this information on the test. If you've already seen sample questions for the test and you have an idea of the question format and style, try to come up with questions of your own that you can answer based on what you're reading. This will give you valuable practice applying your knowledge in the same ways you can expect to on test day.

Good luck and good studying!

Human Origins and Early Civilizations

Paleolithic Period

Lower Paleolithic Period

The Paleolithic period is the earliest period of human development, as well as the longest. It is also commonly referred to as the Old Stone Age. It lasted from about 2 million years ago until between 40,000 and 10,000 years ago. Development during this period was excruciatingly slow. The Paleolithic period is usually divided into three sections: the Lower, Middle, and Upper. The Lower Paleolithic period is characterized by the appearance of stone tools; the chopping tools found at the Olduvai Gorge in Tanzania are from this period, and date back over a million years. They were probably made by Australopithecus, an ancestor of modern humans. Anthropologists have also found stone tools believed to have been made by Homo erectus between 100,000 and 500,000 years ago.

Solutrean and Magdalenian Phase of the Paleolithic Period

During the Upper Paleolithic period, hunters entered Europe from the east and conquered the more primitive cultures living there. These victorious hunters were known as the Solutreans. These people are noted for their fine spearheads which they used to hunt wild horses. The Solutreans were in turn replaced by the Magdelenians, the most advanced phase of the Paleolithic period. The Magdalenians subsisted mainly through fishing and reindeer hunting. They developed extremely precise tools and sophisticated weapons, such as the atlatl: a device that made it possible to throw a spear over a great distance. Most of all, though, the Magdalenians are known for their cave paintings in modern-day France.

Middle and Upper Paleolithic Periods

The Middle Paleolithic period occurred between 100,000 and 40,000 years ago. During this time, the Mousterian culture of Neanderthal men was active in Europe, North Africa, Palestine, and Siberia. These ancestors of modern man lived in caves and had the use of fire. They hunted prehistoric mammals and had slightly more sophisticated tools than their forebears, including crude needles for sewing furs together. These people may have practiced some sort of religion. In the Upper Paleolithic period, Neanderthals were replaced by varieties of Homo sapiens, including Cro-Magnon man and Grimaldi man. A number of diverse cultures flourished during this period, and the first man-made shelters arose. This was also the period in which people first crafted jewelry and illustrated drawings on the walls of caves.

Neolithic Period

The Neolithic period, also known as the New Stone Age, refers to that stage of human cultural evolution in which man developed stone tools, settled in villages, and began making crafts. In order to begin living in towns, man had to learn how to domesticate animals and sustain agriculture; formerly, in the Paleolithic and Mesolithic periods, man had subsisted through hunting, fishing, and gathering. The Neolithic period is said to end when urban civilizations began, or when metal tools or writing began. Because the designation Neolithic depends on these factors, anthropologists date its occurrence differently for different regions and populations. At present, anthropologists believe that the earliest Neolithic culture was in southwest Asia between 8,000 and 6,000 B.C.

Spread of Neolithic Culture

Most anthropologists date the beginning of Neolithic culture at somewhere between 8,000 and 6,000 B.C. It began with the domestication of plants (wheat, barley, and millet) and animals (cattle, sheep, and goats). The Neolithic culture in the valley between the Tigris and Euphrates Rivers gradually evolved into a more urban civilization by 3,500 B.C. Meanwhile, Neolithic cultural advances spread through Europe, the Nile Valley, the Indus Valley, and the Huang He Valley. In these regions, the innovations of the Neolithic period were intermixed with the particulars of the region; in the Huang He region, for instance, rice cultivation was a product of advances in agriculture. By 1,500 B.C., Neolithic culture had spread to Mexico and South America. In these areas, corn, beans, and squash were the major crops.

Mesolithic period

The Mesolithic period, otherwise known as the Middle Stone Age, began roughly 10,000 years ago and ended with the introduction of farming (dates vary by culture). In some areas, the use of farming was already beginning at the end of the Paleolithic era, and therefore there may not be a true Mesolithic period. The most extense examples of this kind of culture are found in Northern Europe, where the end of the Ice Age created much greater changes in the ability to live off of the land. The remains of the Mesolithic period are mainly just middens (rubbish heaps), as well as some deforestation. The people of the Mesolithic period made small tools out of flint; fishing tackle, canoes, and bows have been found at some sites.

Sumerians of Mesopotamia

Mesopotamia, the region between the Tigris and Euphrates Rivers in what is now considered the Middle East, contained several different early civilizations of which the Sumerians were one of the more prominent. They developed the system of writing known as cuneiform, by which they elaborated their theories on mathematics and astronomy. The Sumerians also had a detailed system of laws and traded widely with other groups throughout the region. They even traded with civilizations as far away as Egypt and India. There was no coin or currency system at this time, thus trade was conducted on the barter system, in which goods are exchanged for one another, directly.

Babylonian civilization of Mesopotamia

After the Sumerian civilization declined, the next dominant civilization was Babylon. The Babylonians conquered the Sumerians and established a city on the Euphrates River in approximately 1,750 B.C. One of the most famous Babylonian rulers was Hammurabi, who established the famous Code, an extremely detailed set of laws. This marked the first time that a set of rules governing every aspect of social life was applied to an entire people. The Babylonians are also known for their construction of ziggurats, long pyramid-like structures that were used as religious temples. Over time, the Babylonians acquired a reputation as a sensuous and hedonistic people, and the name Babylon has come to stand for any debauched civilization.

Pyramids of Egypt

The incredible engineering skills of the Egyptians are most famously displayed in the pyramids clustered along the Nile River. These were built roughly between 2,700 and 2,500 B.C. The largest of the structures, the Khufu pyramid at Giza, is estimated to have taken 20 years and 100,000 laborers to construct. Today, it stands at 450 feet; some of its height has been lost to erosion. These pyramids were built as burial sites for the pharaohs, who were believed to continue their rule in the after-life. Peasants worked on the pyramids in exchange for food and shelter. The shape of the pyramids was meant to symbolize the slanting rays of the sun, with sloping sides meant to help the ka (soul) of the pharaoh climb to the sky and join the gods.

Indus Valley civilizations

The Indus River Valley is an area bordered by the Himalayan Mountains in what is now Pakistan. The two great cities of this civilization were Harappa and Mohenjo-Daro, though there were also a large number of smaller communities in the area. The people of this region developed a system of writing, as well as systems of weight and measurement which were useful in trade. They exchanged goods with the people of Mesopotamia in the west as well as with the people of Tibet in the east. The Aryans invaded this region and brought with them iron technology and the Sanskrit language. The introduction of iron tools made it possible to cultivate the forests of the Ganges River Valley in what is now India.

Early cities of Mohenjo-Daro and Harrapa in the Indus Valley

Both the Indus Valley and Egyptian civilizations featured extremely well-planned cities. In the Indus Valley, the cities of Mohenjo-Daro and Harrapa were located along the Indus River, in what is now Pakistan. Each of these cities was built around 2,500 B.C. and housed approximately 30,000 citizens. They were each designed in a grid-like pattern, with streets running east-west and north-south. Both Mohenjo-Daro and Harrapa had bath houses, sewer systems, and organized garbage collection. The structures in these cities were built with oven-fired bricks which made them durable. Unlike in Egypt, where technological advances were used to enhance religious practice, the people of the Indus Valley used their technology to improve sanitation.

Vedic Age

The Vedic Age is the period recounted in the Indian Vedas, the earliest known records of Indian history. The dates of the Vedic age are considered by most to be between 2,000 and 1,000 B.C. The oldest Vedic text is the Rig-Veda, which bears many Indo-Iranian elements. It is a collection of religious hymns and stories and describes a nomadic people who were ruled by a king who depended on their consent. His main duty was to protect the people. Religion in this period primarily consisted of chanting and the performing of sacrifices. During this period, elaborate rules concerning marriage were created, and the rigid social stratification that would become known as the caste system evolved.

Earliest civilization in what would become China

The earliest civilizations in what would become China flourished along the banks of the Huang He (Yellow) River before the year 2,000 B.C. The first Chinese dynasty was the Xia (Hsia), succeeded by the Shang dynasty. In this period, the rulers established an intricate system of government and a comprehensive judiciary. The basic components of this system would be preserved in Chinese civilization for centuries. The distinctive Chinese style of writing also developed during this period. Like Egyptian hieroglyphs, the Chinese pictographs are meant to resemble their definition. Over time, though, the Chinese characters have come to resemble their definitions less and less.

Early civilizations of Mesoamerica and South America

Mesoamerica, which is now known as Central and South America, were both host to developed civilizations 3,000 years before the arrival of Columbus. These civilizations were largely dependent upon water-supported agriculture. The most important crop in the region was maize. The first dominant group in this region, the Olmecs, was based in what is now the gulf coast of eastern Mexico. The Olmecs were known for making large and elaborate stone carvings. There were also major civilizations at this time in what is now Peru. In the Andes Mountains of that region, the Chavin culture developed intricate stone temples and pyramids. These sites have been explored carefully by archaeologists.

World Religions

Hinduism

Hinduism is the traditional religion of India. It is expressed in an individual's philosophy and behavior, rather than in the performance of any specific rituals. Hinduism does not claim a founder, but has evolved slowly over thousands of years; the first Hindu writings date back to the third millennium B.C. There are a few concepts that are common to all permutations of Hinduism, such as the Vedas, which are considered to be the sacred texts of the religion. The chief aim in life for a Hindu is to liberate himself from the cycle of suffering and rebirth. Hindus believe in reincarnation and that a person's conduct in this life will affect his or her position in the next (karma). Although Hinduism is frequently associated with the caste system, the two are actually unrelated.

The Hindu caste system is a means of organizing society. It divides the populace into four groups, each associated with a part of the body of the Hindu god Parusha. The highest class is the brahmins, associated with the mouth of the god. In the original system, the brahmin class was made up of priests. The second caste is the kshatriyas, made up of rulers and soldiers; this caste is associated with the arms of Parusha. Next are the vaishyas, associated with the legs of the god. This caste was composed of landowners, merchants, and artisans. The last group is the shudras, associated with the feet of the god. This caste was composed of servants and slaves. Women do not have a place in the traditional Hindu caste system.

Buddhism

Buddhism was created by Gautama Siddhartha (otherwise known as Buddha) in about 528 B.C. It was in part a response to Hinduism, which Buddha felt had become bloated with worldliness and politics. Traditional Buddhism is based upon the Four Noble Truths: existence is suffering, suffering is caused by desire, an end of suffering will come with Nirvana, and Nirvana will come with the practice of the Eightfold Path. The steps of the Eightfold Path are: right views; right resolve; right speech; right action; right livelihood; right effort; right mindfulness; and right concentration. Buddhism has no deities. Buddhism did not receive any official sanction for a long time, but eventually spread and took hold in India, China, Japan, and elsewhere.

Judaism

Judaism was founded in the 20th century B.C. by a man named Abraham, who was chosen to enter into a covenant with God, whereby he would receive special treatment in exchange for obedience and worship. Abraham then moved to Canaan (present-day Lebanon). Later, his descendants would move to Egypt and be enslaved, before being eventually liberated by God through the leader Moses and reconquering Canaan. Moses received from God a set of strict laws, known as the Ten Commandments. All of this is described in the Torah, the essential Jewish Scripture. There are also several other important books, including the Talmud, and many important commentaries by learned Jewish theologians.

Daoism

Next to Confucianism, Daoism (also Taoism) is the most important philosophy to have emerged out of China. Taoist thought is based on the 6th century B.C. writings of Lao Tzu, specifically on the Tao Te Ching. Lao Tzu was a student of Confucius and taught that individuals should discover the essential nature of things and of themselves, and should not seek to challenge the natural harmony of life. A proper Taoist should be patient and austere. Unlike Confucianism, Daoism contains an element of mysticism and so may be called a religion. Taoism introduced the concept of the yin and yang, the contrasting male and female elements that make up every thing in existence, and which must be harmonized in order to achieve self-realization.

Zoroastrianism

Zoroastrianism was the state religion of Persia during the Sasanian dynasty between the years A.D. 224 and 651. It is based upon the prophecies of Zoroaster (also known as Zarathustra, c. 628-551 B.C.), a Persian who claimed to have encountered the divine being Ahura Mazdah. Zoroastrians believed that the world was composed of good and evil spirits, who are in constant conflict. Fire was sacred to the Zoroastrians. Many of the concepts of Zoroastrianism would be included in Christianity, especially by the Manichean sect, who also saw the world as a struggle between absolute good and absolute evil. Zoroastrianism receded in popularity with the rise of Islam.

Religion in Africa

Sub-Saharan Africa was composed of disparate tribes. Most of Africa practiced animistic religion, in which it is believed that deities are embodied in the animals that people depend upon for food and service. Ritual and participatory worship was important; common activities include drumming, dancing, divination, and sacrifices. These religions typically had well-developed concepts of good and evil; they believed that some evil, disasters and illnesses were produced by witchcraft, and that specialists (known as diviners) were required to combat the power of these malevolent beings. Many African peoples shared an underlying belief in a creator deity, whose power was expressed through the ancestors who founded the tribe. These deceased ancestors were a link between the living and the deities. African tribal religions showed a remarkable resilience when they began to come into contact with monotheistic religions.

Zhou dynasty

The Zhou dynasty, which ran from roughly 1,030 to 221 B.C., is generally considered to be the third Chinese dynasty, after the Shang. The Zhou were brought into power by the commander Wu, who declared that the decadent Shang monarchs had forfeited the mandate of heaven (in other words, God's approval of their reign). The Zhou dynasty is generally divided into two parts; the Western Zhou ran a feudal-type state in the central plain and the area around the Yellow River. The later Eastern Zhou had a more difficult time maintaining control of rival states within its control. The Zhou dynasty was the period in which Chinese civilization spread to most parts of Asia. Both Confucius and Lao Tzu were active during this period. China became the preeminent state during this period.

Persia

Persia is the European name for the region that is now Iran. This area has been the site of a number of vibrant cultures. The Medes were the first to develop there, lasting from approximately 700 to 549 B.C., when they were expelled by the army of Cyrus. This great king then established the Achaemenid dynasty, which itself was destroyed by Alexander the Great in 330 B.C. After this, a succession of peoples including the Parthians—rivals to Rome—inhabited the region, until a durable Sasanian dynasty was established in A.D. 224. Persia was in constant conflict with the Byzantine Empire, and would eventually be overtaken by the Arabs in the seventh century A.D.

Ancient Israel

Around the year 1,020 B.C., the Hebrew leader Saul became the first king of the nation known as Israel. He was succeeded by King David, who conquered the important city of Jerusalem. In the 10th century B.C., King Solomon built the first Jewish Temple in Jerusalem, which was used to house the Ark of the Covenant which contained the twin tablets of commandments and other religious artifacts. Israel would be taken over by the Assyrians in the 8th century B.C., and later by the Babylonians. Finally, in 538 B.C., the Persian King Cyrus allowed the Jews to return to Jerusalem and rebuild the Temple. Israel would subsequently be taken over by the Greeks under Alexander, and later by the Romans under Pompey Magnus.

Nok culture

One of the most successful cultures of the African Iron Age was the Nok culture. The Nok developed ironworking technology before anyone else, and also created a rich artistic culture that spread throughout the West African forest region. The Nok were mainly active between the 5th and the 1st centuries B.C. Their creation of iron farm implements made it possible for farmers to develop surplus crops, and thus urban centers could develop. This increase in agricultural productivity also made it possible for there to be more specialization of labor. Therefore, not only were civilizations more stable, but they were also better able to protect themselves, as they now had both better weapons made of iron and more time to train warriors.

Classical Civilizations

Mauryan Empire

The Mauryan Empire lasted approximately between the years 321 and 185 B.C. in India. It was established by the powerful leader Chandragupta Maurya, and featured a strong military and an efficient bureaucracy. The Mauryan empire eventually spread as far west of the Indus River as present-day Afghanistan. At its greatest expansion, the Mauryan empire comprised almost the entirety of what is now India. The leader Ashoka (c. 272-232 B.C.) converted to Buddhism, and his rule was prosperous for rich and poor alike. After the death of Ashoka, however, the Mauryan Empire splintered, as the southern lands sought autonomy and the northern lands were subject to constant foreign invasions.

Han dynasty

The Han dynasty ran from approximately 206 B.C. to A.D. 220. It began when a peasant, Liu Pang, led a successful insurrection against the Qin dynasty leaders. The Han shifted the capital of China to Changan (Xian). This was the period in which Confucianism became the dominant political and social ideology in China. The Han developed a code of laws and a form of government based upon the proper Confucian relations between king and subject, husband and wife, and father and son. The Han dynasty saw China accrue fantastic wealth, and become one of the most sophisticated and resplendent countries the world has seen. Eventually, though, peasant revolts weakened the Han and made them susceptible to overthrow.

Greece

Athens in ancient Greece

Ancient Greece was dominated by two city-states, Athens and Sparta. These two had very distinct cultures. Athens was a coastal city with a democratic form of government which amassed wealth by trading overseas. Athens is also known as the city that gave life to philosophy and the arts. Socrates engaged in his famous dialogues in the streets of Athens, and though he was eventually executed by the Athenian government for supposedly corrupting the youth, his thoughts achieved immortality in the writings of his student Plato. In turn, Plato's student Aristotle developed a strict form of reasoning that has formed the basis of much subsequent Western thought. Athens is also renowned for the architectural marvel that is the Parthenon.

Sparta in ancient Greece

While Athens was known for its devotion to the arts and its democratic form of government, its rival city-state Sparta was devoted to agriculture and the military. Sparta was not located on the coast, and therefore the Spartans had little contact with distant peoples. Spartan society was governed by a strict class system. Most people (helots) worked the land of other people as virtual serfs. In the upper classes, participation in military training was compulsory. Indeed, Spartan youths left their families to begin military training at a young age. The Spartans did not produce any noteworthy philosophers, but as a culture they stressed the good of the group over that of the individual. This is in stark contrast to most Athenian thought, which celebrates the achievements of the individual.

Greece in the Periclean and Hellenistic Ages

The Periclean Age in Greece, so named because Pericles was the leader of Athens during the period, took place in the fifth century B.C. It was during this period that most of the great contributions to Western culture were made, including the philosophy of Socrates, the medical work of Hippocrates, and the great dramatic works of Aeschlyus, Sophocles, and Euripides. The Hellenistic Age (4th century B.C.), on the other hand, is more commonly known for the military conquests made by Alexander the Great. If it were not for the conquests of Alexander during the Hellenistic Age, many of the innovations and achievements of the Periclean Age may not have had such a great influence on the West. It should be noted that the Hellenistic Age was not without its own great thinkers; in fact, Alexander studied as a boy under Aristotle.

Major wars of Greece in the Periclean and Hellenistic Ages

During the Age of Pericles, an alliance of Greek city-states was challenged by the mighty Persians. Miraculously, the outnumbered Greeks were able to defeat the Persians at Thermopylae and Marathon, and staved off conquest. The war with the Persians impoverished the Greeks, however, and increased rivalries among the city-states. In Athens, the requirements for citizenship were loosened, though slavery remained. Conflict between Sparta and Athens culminated in the Peloponnesian War, won by Sparta. Eventually, the whole of Greece would be conquered by Philip of Macedon, who allowed the Greeks to maintain their culture and traditions. Alexander the Great was the son of Philip and became the master of an empire larger than any the world had ever seen. During his reign, he united many disparate peoples through a common law and exchange policy. He died at the age of 33, and his empire was divided into three parts amongst his generals.

Roman Republic

Roman civilization dates from the founding of the city in 753 B.C. until the defeat of the last Emperor, Romulus Augustus, in A.D. 476. The republic itself lasted from the overthrow of the monarchy in 509 B.C. until the empowering of the first Emperor, Octavian Augustus, in 27 B.C. The area along the Tiber River where Rome would be built was previously inhabited by a group known as the Etruscans. Rome took its name from the legendary Romulus, who is said to have founded it after triumphing over his brother Remus. The basic structure of Roman society consisted of patricians at the top of the social hierarchy, who were descendants of the founders of the republic and often wealthy. Beneath the patricians were the plebeians, which consisted of all other freemen. Finally, at the bottom of the social hierarchy were slaves. Women were not included in most social or economic business, although a Roman woman's rights were often significantly preferable to her contemporaries in other civilizations. The Roman Republic, which was the first political arrangement of Rome, was led by two consuls who were chosen annually. The Consuls presided over the Senate, made up of a permanent group of those who had been previously elected to a high-ranking magistracy (originally primarily patrician in composition); and the Assembly, which was solely for the plebeians. Rome had extensive laws covering individual and property rights.

Greece, Gaul and Spain

After defeating Carthage once and for all, Rome met little resistance as it continued to acquire more territory. This was partly due to the superiority of Roman weaponry, and in part because the Romans were good at bringing conquered peoples into the fold. Rome typically allowed conquered people to maintain their native cultures, so long as they paid tribute to Rome. Rome defeated the Macedonians and took Greece, then conquered large portions of Gaul (France) and Spain. The vastness of the Roman Empire necessitated some advances in infrastructure technology. Romans are justly famous or their solid and durable roads and aqueducts (systems for delivering water), many of which survive today.

Punic Wars

The first real challenge to the territorial expansion of Rome was the city of Carthage, located across the Mediterranean in North Africa. Carthage was founded by the Phoenicians. There were three major conflicts, known as the Punic Wars, fought between Rome and Carthage. Rome won the First

Punic War, and acquired Sicily in the process. The Carthaginian effort in the Second Punic War was led by Hannibal and included his famous crossing of the Alps. Hannibal was quite successful in Italy, but a combination of a war of attrition throughout Italy and the counterattacks on Carthaginian holdings in Spain and the city of Carthage itself by the Romans forced Hannibal to retreat to North Africa to defend Carthage. In the Third Punic War, Rome finally destroyed Carthage; in fact, it is often rumored that the victorious Romans burned Carthage to the ground and then salted the fields of their vanquished foe, a tribute to the Senator Cato the Elder's repeated cry at the end of various speeches of "*Ceterum censeo Carthaginem esse delendam*" ("Moreover, I have determined that Carthage must be destroyed").

Roman Triumvirate

After the assassination of Caesar in 44 B.C., Rome was mired in chaos. Those who had conspired to kill Caesar had hoped to return to the republican form of government, but instead another trio of leaders came to the fore, this time as a governmental commission of "three men for reconstituting the Republic," known as the Triumvirate. The Triumvirate was composed of Marc Antony, one of Caesar's greatest generals and a Consul at the time; Octavius, the nephew and testamentary heir of Caesar; and Marcus Aemilius Lepidus, a third wheel who was quickly made a non-entity. While Octavius stayed in Rome, Antony left for Egypt, where he stayed for a time as the guest and lover of Cleopatra. Eventually, infighting between Octavius and Antony led the former to mount a campaign against Egypt. When they realized that they were defeated, Antony and Cleopatra committed suicide to avoid the shame of being paraded in Octavian's triumph. Lepidus, having been marginalized, Octavius (now known as Augustus) became the first Emperor.

Grand Alliance of Julius Caesar in Rome

As Rome continued to expand, class conflicts developed between the nobility and the poor. In this era of unrest, it became possible for individual leaders to claim more power than the law had allowed previously. In 60 B.C., the famous general Julius Caesar formed a three-person alliance (often mis-termed the "First Triumvirate") to govern Rome. The other two members were Gnaeus Pompey Magnus and Marcus Licinius Crassus. During this period, Caesar led a successful campaign against the Gauls (a people in modern-day France) and made himself richer than the entire Roman State on the proceeds from his conquest. After Crassus was killed in battle, Caesar pushed Pompey out and assumed total control of Rome, crowning himself dictator-for life. Though Caesar was very popular with the mob, his decision to claim lifelong power alienated him from the nobility in the Senate. He was assassinated by a group of senators, led by Marcus Iunius Brutus, in 44 B.C.

Pax Romana

After the ascension of Augustus, Rome entered a period of relative tranquility. Augustus dubbed this era, which lasted about forty years, the Pax Romana. Rome remained an empire, although the conquered peoples were able to obtain Roman citizenship without having to forfeit their native customs. It was at this period that Rome reached its greatest geographic proportions, stretching all the way up to present-day Scotland. This was also the greatest period for Roman artistic achievement; both Virgil and Ovid were active during the Pax Romana, and, indeed, the Aeneid of Virgil was written in part to glorify Augustus. It was at this time that the polytheist religion of Rome was challenged first by the Judaism of the conquered Hebrews, and later by the early Christians.

Rise of Christianity

Early Christianity was a mass of competing doctrines, including various groups such as the Gnostics and Arians who all sought to have their view legitimized as the truth. Eventually, the orthodox church through an ecumenical council of bishops created in the fourth century A.D. the canon of

New Testament texts which exists today. The apostles had created a hierarchy of bishops, priests, and deacons who stressed obedience to duly constituted church authority. By the middle of the second century, Christianity began to attract intellectuals in the Roman Empire. Although Christians were still liable to be persecuted in the farther reaches of the empire, many turned to the Church as the empire crumbled, as the Church was all that was left of civilization, and would rebuild Europe over the next millennium.

Constantine and the Christians

The Roman Emperor Constantine, in response to the inconvenient vastness of his dominion, established an eastern capital: Constantinople, in A.D. 330. Having received a sign in the heavens which promised him victory over his rivals for the office of Emperor should he convert to Christianity, Constantine famously issued the Edict of Milan, in which he called for the end of the persecution of Christians, after a sound victory as promised. After this act, Christianity flourished in the Roman Empire and became the official religion of the state. A movement called monasticism developed within the religion, advocating the renunciation of worldly goods in favor of contemplation and prayer. After the death of Constantine, the empire once again proved unwieldy for one man, and therefore it split as it had previously, with the western half being governed from Rome, and the eastern half from Constantinople. This arrangement would prove untenable, however; a Germanic tribe of barbarians eventually sacked Rome, and the western Roman capital fell in A.D. 476.

Aksum

Aksum (Axom), a town in what is now northern Ethiopia, was the capital city of one of Africa's most powerful kingdoms between the first and sixth centuries A.D. The kings of Aksum were said to have descended from Menelik, one of the sons of the famous King Solomon. These people controlled almost all of the trade on the Red Sea and made tremendous profit on the exchange of ivory. In the 4th century A.D., Aksum eliminated the kingdom of Kush and became the predominant power in Africa. It was also during this century that Aksum was Christianized; it remains a hub of Ethiopian Christianity to this day. In its later stages, Aksum's control extended into southern Arabia, and would eventually give way to the Persians and the Arabs.

Kush

Kush was a powerful African kingdom that lasted in some form from 2,000 B.C. until A.D. 350. For a long time, Kush was based around the city of Kerma, in what is now the Sudan. Kushites became wealthy because of their mineral resources and because of their advantageous location in the northwest corner of Africa where they were at the crossroads of several intercontinental trade routes. There was a great deal of contact between Kush and Egypt in this period. In 767 B.C., King Kashta of Kush defeated the Egyptians, and the Kushites had control of the entire Nile Valley. Kush would soon be weakened by the Assyrians, however, and would eventually fall prey to the Romans; in A.D. 350, the new capital of Kush, Meroe, was sacked.

Huns

The Huns were a nomadic people who moved east across central Asia during the 4th century A.D. The Huns were divided into several branches: the White Huns overran the Sasanian Empire and conquered many cities in the northern part of the Indian subcontinent; another group roamed eastern Europe and established a strong empire on the Hungarian Plain around A.D. 400. The Huns were known for their amazing horsemanship and for being aggressive on the battlefield. It was under the guidance of Attila (440s) that the Huns reached their highest level of prominence. During this period, they collected tribute from many of the areas within the Roman Empire. Soon after the death of Attila, however, the Huns became complacent and lost most of their territory.

Postclassical Civilizations

Tang dynasty

The Tang dynasty was in control of China from A.D. 618 to 907. One of the main projects pursued by the Tang rulers was the unification of the far-flung and diverse Chinese states. The early portion of the Tang dynasty is considered one of the high points in Chinese history; the economy and the arts both flourished. Under the leadership of Tang generals, Chinese soldiers would claim parts of Afghanistan, Tibet, and Korea. The Tang were also somewhat unique as Chinese leaders in that they encouraged the introduction of foreign ideas into Chinese culture. Printing was invented in China during this period, and thus ideas could be disseminated much more easily. The end of the Tang dynasty came after a period of internal governmental conflict.

Song dynasty

The Song dynasty of China lasted between the years A.D. 960 and 1279. The Song rulers are credited with reuniting many portions of China that had become disjointed. Historians usually distinguish between the Northern and the Southern Song. The leaders of the Song dynasty made a deliberate effort to reduce the emphasis on military conquest; instead, they focused on developing China's civil service. The Song dynasty saw a rejuvenation of Confucian philosophy in China, as well as a renewed interest in the arts. Some people compare the Song dynasty with the European Renaissance. The Song was the only dynasty in China not to be ended by internal conflict; the Song were ousted by a rebel leader instead.

Mongols

The Mongols, who descended from the Huns, were a nomadic group that roamed east central Asia. Around the year A.D. 1206, the various Mongol tribes were united under Genghis Khan, whose empire then stretched from the Black Sea to the Pacific Ocean, and from Tibet to Siberia. After the death of Genghis, the Mongol lands were divided up. This did not, however, slow expansion; Mongols eventually controlled parts of Iran as well. Kublai Khan was another prominent Mongol leader; he destroyed the Song dynasty in China and replaced it with the Yuan. By the 14th century, the Mongol Empire was beginning to disintegrate. Like many of its kind, it proved too large to govern. The Ming and subsequently the Qing dynasties put the remaining Mongols under Chinese control.

Ming dynasty

The Ming dynasty lasted in China from A.D. 1368 to 1644. This dynasty was established by a Buddhist monk, Zhu Yuanzhang, who quickly became obsessed with consolidating power in the central government and was known for the brutality with which he achieved his ends. It was during the Ming dynasty that China developed and introduced its famous civil service examinations, rigorous tests on the Confucian classics. The future of an ambitious Chinese youth depended on his performance on this exam. The capital was transferred from Nanjing to Beijing during this period, and the Forbidden City was constructed inside the new capital. The Ming period, despite its constant expansionary wars, also continued China's artistic resurgence; the porcelain of this period is especially admired.

Byzantine Empire

The eastern half of the Roman Empire became known as the Byzantine Empire. After the fall of Rome, the Emperor Justinian led successfully from Constantinople for a number of years. The Justinian era is especially remembered for the contributions to law and religious art work, in particular the development of mosaics. In the years after the fall of Rome, the Catholic Christian Church gradually rose to fill the power vacuum. In what had been the western Roman Empire, the Church acted completely independent of any political body, while even in the Byzantine Empire the Church was increasing in power. Only the influence of the Byzantine Emperor kept the Church from being the most powerful group in all of Europe.

Steppe Peoples and Seljuk Turks

Between the years A.D. 1,000 and 1,450, invaders from the steppes conquered parts of Asia, the Middle East, and Europe. These people had originally been nomads, but in this period they began to settle and become tradesmen. The clans that made up this group were loosely based on family ties; once they became stationary, they began to appoint powerful chiefs for leadership support. Near A.D. 1,000, the Seljuk Turks moved from Central Asia into the Middle East. This group then controlled the trade routes between Asia, Africa, and Europe, and charged tolls on these routes, building an empire with their wealth. In 1071, the Seljuk Turks defeated the Byzantines at the Battle of Manzikert; a Christian defeat which would be part of the motivation for the First Crusade. The Seljuk Turks were known as excellent fighters and mediocre rulers; local leaders frequently ignored the central government and fought one another for control of land. This infighting weakened the group until they became prey to new nomadic invaders from Central Asia.

Emergence of Russia

In the Middle Ages Russia had a complicated and inefficient system of succession, which meant that the various lands were constantly being fought over and authority was often dubious. For a long time, Russia was dominated by the Mongols (Tatars), who kept the local governments weak in order to continue receiving tributes. Moscow as able to parlay loyalty to the Tatars and colonization of other feudal estates into a great deal of power during this period. Supported by their Tatar overlords, the Muscovite princes were able to partition off their new lands in such a way that it became very difficult for nobles to consolidate their land holdings, which prevented any wealthy lords from ever challenging the princes of Moscow.

Poland and Hungary

During the Middle Ages, a number of different leaders tried to unite the various lands of Poland. These attempts were always defeated by the nobility, who preferred the country to be an oligarchy rather than a monarchy. Poland was also much involved during this period in a battle with the Teutonic knights over the Baltic coastline. Hungary was a feudal state by the beginning of the 14th century, and the various patches of land which constituted the country were ruled as if they were independent. Bishops in the Eastern Orthodox Church were among the largest landholders. Ostensibly, the nobility was in charge of the defense of the Hungarian people, though they rarely supplied the money and material for war.

Islamic civilization

After the formation of Islam in the 7th century A.D., it took 3 or 4 centuries to develop the institutional structures of the religion. Islamic law was created, and a new class of Muslim religious leaders and scholars emerged who took a prominent place in society. The Islamic civilization drew elements from its surroundings, namely the culture of the Greeks, Iranians, Christians, Jews, and Zoroastrians. At first, the Islamic Empire was ruled by a single caliph and a small Arab elite. As the empire expanded, however, this became untenable and the lands were divided into a number of independent political entities. Also, factions began to emerge among Muslims, most notably between the Sunnis and Shiites, who rivaled over the true successor to Muhammad, among other issues. Because the entire Islamic world operated with a common system of trade, it quickly became very wealthy.

ORIGINS AND EXPANSION OF ISLAM

The religion of Islam was founded by the prophet Muhammad in A.D. 610. Islam is a monotheistic religion based on the Koran, a book of scripture according to the muslim god, Allah. The practice of Islam is based on "Five Pillars": faith in Allah, a pilgrimage to the city of Mecca; a yearly fast during the month of Ramadan; the giving of alms; and prayer five times a day. Muhammad also asserted that Islam should be spread throughout the world. Indeed, as the Christian Church was becoming the dominant factor in Europe, Islam was spreading throughout North Africa, the Middle East, parts of Asia, and even Spain. The simultaneous ascensions of Christianity and Islam inevitably led to conflict, most notably in the Crusades.

ANCIENT MALI

Today, Mali is the largest nation in west Africa. Indeed, throughout African history Mali has been a major power. Until the 11th century, it was a part of the empire of Ghana, a wealthy trading nation. Mali would eventually rise to prominence in its own right. The economy of Mali was based upon the rich mineral resources (especially gold) of the region. Mali reached its highest prominence during the reign of Mansa Musa (A.D. 1312-7). This ruler introduced Islam to his people, which at this time lived as far north as Morocco. The city of Timbuktu became a cultural center for the region, as well as a crossroads for trade routes that stretched across the Sahara. Over time, internal disputes would divide Mali into several smaller kingdoms.

ANCIENT GHANA

Beginning in the 7th century A.D., Ghana was a major trading power in west Africa. It was mainly located in the areas that are now known as Mali and Mauritania. The people of Ghana grew rich by exchanging ivory and gold from the south and salt from the north. Eventually, Ghana would become an empire, and would collect lavish tributes from all of the lands within its control. In the 11th century, the capital of Ghana was Kumbi. In 1076, however, Kumbi fell to the Almoravids, a Muslim tribe. The whole of Ghana would eventually be subsumed into the burgeoning empire of Mali.

SONGHAI EMPIRE

The Songhai empire flourished in west Africa between the 14th and 16th centuries. Centered in the valley of the Niger River, the Songhai were first organized by Christian Berbers in the 7th century. Four hundred years later, they established their capital at Gao and became an Islamic nation. Except for a brief period in which they were ruled by the empire of Mali, the Songhai controlled over a thousand miles along the Niger. Like most of the African powers, the Songhai made their money through trade. Muhammad I, who ruled from 1493 to 1528, expanded the empire to its greatest area. One of the weaknesses of the Songhai, however, was that they did not have a traditional means of succession, and thus frequent infighting among the powerful eventually led to the empire's demise.

FEUDALISM

Feudalism was the system of social and economic organization that developed in Europe in the Middle Ages: roughly A.D. 750 to 1300. Feudalism is characterized by rigid hierarchies among the various classes. At the top of the hierarchy was the king, and below him lords, who oversaw a smaller area of land. Below the lords were noblemen who had been granted control over farmland in exchange for their pledge of allegiance to the king. These noblemen were known as vassals and subvassals. The land managed by each vassal was known as a fief, and the home of the vassal was known as the manor. Each manor and the community surrounding it comprised a self-sufficient unit. The laws of primogeniture were enforced at this time, meaning that the ownership of the fief would descend to the firstborn son of the lord. Finally, the land was actually cultivated either by peasants or serfs; peasants were free farmers, while serfs were basically slaves who were forced to work for the lord and were bound to their lands.

CHARLEMAGNE

The emergence of the feudal system in western Europe meant that instead of a centralized power, there were many local authorities. Charlemagne (A.D. 742-814) was a Germanic leader who tried to unify the former western Roman Empire. In A.D. 800, Pope St. Leo III crowned Charlemagne Emperor of Rome during Christmas Mass at St. Peter's Basilica in Rome, establishing a political relationship with the Church that would last throughout the Middle Ages. Charlemagne allocated a great deal of power to regional leaders, and did not tax his subjects. For this reason, he was unable to make many internal improvements during his reign. Nevertheless, Charlemagne is credited with promoting the arts, especially within the thriving monasteries, without which much of antiquity would not have been transcribed and thus preserved. After the death of Charlemagne, his lands were divided up among his three grandsons according to the Treaty of Verdun.

END OF FEUDALISM

In the late 13th century, increased contact between regions and greater representation in government culminated in a number of peasant revolts and serf uprisings. During this period, members of the clergy became even more secular and open in their greed for fame and power. This alienated many common citizens from the Church. The invention of gunpowder also changed the social arrangements in Western Europe; fewer noblemen were willing to participate in combat, and so the code of chivalry gave way to mercenary soldiers. Noblemen largely turned their attention to acquiring some of the fantastic wealth available in trade. The quality that men strived for in these days was called virtue, meaning a solemn dedication to the arts and sciences.

HOLY ROMAN EMPIRE

The Holy Roman Empire was the name given to the holdings of Otto the Great in 962, who had unified the central area of Charlemagne's empire. As in Charlemagne's day, this was a disparate group of territories, and proved difficult to govern. Otto incorporated the Church into his government, though he continually sought to minimize its power. One of the legacies of Otto's reign would be the rivalry between the Church and state. Gradually, the Church leaders acquired power, until they were exercising great control over the day-to-day activities of most citizens. Perhaps inevitably, this great power began to corrupt many of the Church's leaders. Indicative of the state of the Church was the often unpunished offense of simony, in which prestigious and important offices were bought and sold.

FAITH AND LEARNING IN WESTERN EUROPE DURING THE LATE MIDDLE AGES

Surprising though it may seem, one of the best things that happened to Christian thought during the Middle Ages was its contact with Islam. The complex philosophies of Muslim scholars helped spur the evolution of Christian theology. These in addition to the rediscovery of ancient philosophers such as Aristotle led Christians to begin to glorify reason as the God-given tool for investigating religious faith. Many assertions made by the new rational theologians, however, were dubbed heresy by many Church leaders, as more and more Christian thinkers were bemoaning the materialistic ways of the Church leaders. One of the leading Christian thinkers of the Middle Ages was St. Thomas Aquinas, whose Summa Theologica outlined rational explanations for the belief in God and in the miracles of Christianity.

Formation of Universities in the Middle Ages

The rapid evolution in Christian thought that took place during the Middle Ages gave rise to the formation of the first universities. For the first time in Western Europe, young men would move to large cities to study theology, law, and medicine at formal institutions. In addition to this trend, the academic method known as scholasticism was developed, in which scholars would use logic and deductive reasoning in order to analyze a work or determine something of an abstract nature. Among the so-called scholastics, two schools of thought developed: those scholars who adhered to the ideas of Plato were known as realists, and those who followed Aristotle were known as nominalists. The word "realist" is somewhat confusing when used to refer to the work of Plato, who believed that our perceptions of objects were merely perceptions of the barest shadows of their reality. Another development of Christianity in this period was mysticism; Christian mystics believed that they could achieve union with God through self-denial, contemplative prayer, and alms-giving.

Western Europe in the 12th and 13th Centuries

In the 12th century A.D., the various fiefs in Western Europe increasingly came into contact with one another. As advances in transportation technology made trade with distant neighbors possible, there developed more necessity for specialization. Rather than be entirely self-sufficient, lords found it was more economically advantageous to perfect the cultivation of one crop and exchange that for everything else. As trade became more important, so did the merchants in towns, known as burghers, who wielded considerable political power. Trade arrangements led to alliances between various towns, and the whole of Western Europe became more homogenous. The distinction between classes also became much less pronounced during this period. There were drawbacks, however: the increasing number of people in towns as well as the more frequent travel between towns contributed, no doubt, to the bubonic plague epidemic of the mid-14th century.

Germany, Italy, and France in the 13th Century

During the 13th century, France was transformed from a group of disparate fiefs into a centralized monarchy by Philip Augustus (Philip II). His heir, Philip IV, would establish the Estates General, a governing body composed of representatives from each province. The Estates General contained noblemen as well as wealthy commoners. Meanwhile, Germany endured an interregnum, or period between kings, after the ruler died without a clear successor. Italy, as well, spent this period as a collection of strong and independent townships. In a decentralized state, it became easier for wealthy merchants to wield power. In Germany, the Hanseatic League, an association of merchants, set regional trade policy.

Magna Carta

England, unlike many of the other regions of Western Europe, had been accustomed to a strong monarchy. This tradition was challenged in A.D. 1215, when noblemen forced King John to sign the Magna Carta, a document which gave feudal rights back to the nobles and extended the rule of law to the middle-class burghers. The Magna Carta made the formation of the Houses of Parliament possible. Over time, Parliament would evolve into a two-house structure: the House of Lords which contained nobles and clergy and the House of Commons which contained knights and burghers. The House of Lords was mainly occupied with legal questions, while the House of Commons dealt mainly in economic issues.

Crisis in the Western church (1300)

Babylon captivity and schism

After the death of Pope Boniface VIII, King Philip IV of France persuaded the College of Cardinals to select a French archbishop as the next pope. This pope, Clement V, moved the papacy to Avignon, France, where it would remain for 67 years. Debate raged during this period as to whether a pope could be legitimate in any city other than Rome. Also, Clement's court became notorious for its extravagance. In 1378, a new pope was chosen; an Italian, who chose the name Urban VI to indicate that he planned on keeping the papacy in Rome. Upset with Urban's policy, 13 French cardinals selected a new pope, the French-speaking Clement VII. Now, there were two popes, and each one declared the other illegitimate. This confusion lasted from 1378 until 1417, with the Pope in Rome and an antipope in Avignon.

Papal bull "Unam Sanctam"

Around the year 1300, the power of the Pope in political affairs was weakening because of the rise of strong monarchs and a spirit of nationalism. Pope Boniface VIII attempted to force kings to obey him, but was unsuccessful. In response, Boniface issued a papal bull in 1296 that instructed King Philip IV of France to not tax the church; Philip ignored this command. Boniface would not relent, and issued the bull "Unam Sanctam," in which he declared that there are two powers on the earth, the temporal and the spiritual, with the latter always superior, and that there is no salvation outside of loyalty to the Roman Pontiff. Once again, Philip refused the claims of the Pope, and decided to silence him by having him kidnapped and brought to France. Boniface was able to escape captivity, but died soon afterward. This significantly weakened the political authority of the papacy.

Effects of the Black Death and Johannes Gutenberg

Towards the end of the Middle Ages, two events greatly shaped future events. The *bubonic plague*, also known as the *Black Death*, killed between 30 and 60% of the European population. The influx of people to squalid cities made the rapid spread of this disease possible. The seemingly random devastation caused by the disease caused many people to question their faith, and the power of the Church suffered as a result. The other monumental event was the invention of the printing press by *Johannes Gutenberg* in about 1436. This invention was used first to produce a cheap copy of the Bible. Soon, though, printing presses with movable type were being used to print all sorts of things, and the literacy rate in Europe rose dramatically. It immediately became possible to disseminate ideas quickly.

Hundred Years' War

England made a claim on the French throne in 1337, and the result was a war (or series of wars) that lasted for 116 years. France was angry, in return, that England had not upheld its feudal obligations to the French throne, to whom the English king was technically a distant vassal. France had the support of the Pope, but England used the innovation of the longbow to score some significant victories. It was during this war that the charismatic figure Joan of Arc emerged. Joan was a French peasant who led troops to several unlikely victories after being visited by God. Her deeds rallied the spirits of the French, and France eventually won. The catastrophic losses suffered by both sides had major consequences: England withdrew from contention as a land power, electing instead to develop a navy; in France, Louis IX—St. Louis—took advantage of the chaos to consolidate power in the monarchy.

Mayas

The Mayas were based in the Mexico's Yucatan Peninsula, Tabasco, and Chiapas, as well as in what is now Guatemala and Honduras. Between the years A.D. 200 and 950, they developed a sophisticated civilization, with complex religions, architecture, arts, engineering, and astronomy. The Mayas did have a form of hieroglyphic writing, but most of their history and folklore was preserved orally. The Mayas are responsible for creating an extremely accurate calendar and for first conceiving of the number zero. The Mayan civilization was supported by agriculture, but it was run by a class of priests and warriors. In the 9th century, the Mayans were overrun by Toltecs from the north, who created the legend of the feathered serpent Quetzalcoatl.

Mayan Religion

The Mayans conceived of the universe as a flat, square earth, whose four corners and center were dominated by a god. Above the sky, there were 13 levels, and below were 9 underworlds, each dominated by a god. The sun and moon, deities in their own right, passed through all of these levels every day. Each male god had a female goddess counterpart. The Mayans also had patron gods and goddesses for various occupations and classes. Mayan rulers had religious powers. Religious ritual often entailed human sacrifice and self-mutilation. The Mayans also played a ritual ball game that had religious importance; the losers of this game stood to lose their lives. Mayans developed their cities as tributes to the gods.

Aztecs

When the Toltec empire had been eradicated around the year 1150, the power in Mesoamerica shifted to the valley of Mexico, around three lakes. By about 1325, the Aztecs had seized control of this area. The Aztec civilization was organized into city-states, much like early medieval Europe; political intrigue and state marriages were as common among the Aztecs as among the French. The Aztecs were known as fierce warriors and were hated by their neighbors because of their brutality. According to legend, the Aztecs settled in Tenochtitlan after a scout saw an eagle with a serpent in its beak perched on a cactus there. The Aztecs formed alliances based on threats and forced tributes.

Incas

The Incas inhabited a huge area, from present-day Ecuador to central Chile to the eastern side of the Andes Mountains. The Incas territory expanded especially after the 14th century A.D. The Incas were engaged in frequent conflicts with rival groups, and they frequently enslaved the groups that they defeated. They eventually formed a permanent underclass of serfs in order to ensure that the lands of the military leaders would be cultivated. Incas typically dispersed rival groups in order to prevent being attacked. The Incan religion contained a god in heaven, a cult of ancestors, and a number of sacred objects and places. The Incas called themselves the children of the Sun.

Feudalism in Japan

Feudalism developed in Japan after wars in the 11th century left much of the land in the control of military leaders. These men did not actually own the land, but a complex set of rights were given to them, whereby they had the exclusive right to cultivate and profit from the land. Many Japanese were disenchanted with the central government at this time, and so the idea of powerful regional leaders appealed to them. A code of ethics specific to feudalism emerged, and Japanese peasants were required to pledge loyalty to a particular lord rather than to a political ideal. One particular feudal administration, the Minamoto, acquired almost the entirety of Japan and replaced the central government for most people.

Practice Test

Practice Questions

1. Which of the following aspects of civilization were first developed as early as 5,000 years ago?

a. Centralized governments
b. The Dialogues of Socrates
c. Building of the Parthenon
d. The recording of the Torah

2. When did the "Father of Medicine," after whom today's oath "First do no harm" live?

a. After the development of Euclidean geometry
b. Before Archimedes's famous bathtub discovery
c. When Mexico's Temple of the Sun was erected
d. After Aristotle's completed his Western philosophy

3. Which of the following events in ancient history occurred earliest in time?

a. The suicide of Cleopatra, the last Pharaoh of Egypt
b. The assassination of Roman Emperor, Julius Caesar
c. The revolt of the Maccabees of Israel against Seleucids
d. The slaves' rebellion against Rome led by Spartacus

4. Which of the following events affecting the Roman Empire and Christianity came latest?

a. Widespread Roman persecution of Christians first began
b. Gothic and Frankish tribes escalated invasions in Europe
c. Emperor Constantine the Great passed the Edict of Milan
d. The Council of Nicaea defined Orthodox Christian beliefs

5. Among these actions by European ancestor tribes contributing to the fall of the Roman Empire, which one took place last?

a. The Visigoth King Alaric I sacked the city of Rome
b. Mongol Attila the Hun invaded Roman provinces
c. The tribe known as the Vandals destroyed Rome
d. Ostrogoths Theodoric founded his Kingdom of Italy

6. How long did the period known as the Middle Ages, in Europe, last?

a. 100 years
b. 500 years
c. 1,000 years
d. 1,200 years

7. Who was most responsible for the development of medieval universities in the 11th century?

a. King Charlemagne
b. Pope Gregory VII
c. Robert Sorbon
d. John Balliol

8. Which of the following did China's Han Dynasty and Europe's Western Roman Empire share in common?

a. Both suffered population loss from plagues
b. Both reigned for roughly the same duration
c. Both were succeeded by stronger empires
d. Both fell without the influence of income taxes

9. Which statement is true about medieval Byzantium?

a. It endured 11 centuries after Constantinople's founding
b. It was primarily Muslim in its religion until the 7th century
c. It was highly unstable in character during medieval times
d. Its strongest times were noted for intellectual advances

10. Which statement most accurately describes the relationship of medieval Byzantium to the Renaissance in Europe?

a. Medieval Byzantium delayed the advent of the European Renaissance
b. Medieval Byzantium prepared the way for the European Renaissance
c. Medieval Byzantium had no relationship to the European Renaissance
d. Medieval Byzantium's unity opposed the diversity of the Renaissance

11. What was true about the Eastern and Western versions of early Christianity?

a. The government of the Roman Empire did not recognize Christianity in the 5th century
b. Eastern and Western Europe's Christianity were essentially the same in the 4th century
c. The Western Christian Church had a centralized leadership; the Eastern Church did not
d. Regardless of locations, members of the Eastern and Western Churches all spoke Latin

12. Which of the following is true of the Great Schism?

a. It occurred in European churches during the 10th century A.D.
b. It was the separation of the Protestants from the Catholics
c. It established separation of Christians from non-Christians
d. It created Roman Catholic and Eastern Orthodox Churches

13. Which of the following factors contributing to the change from the Medieval to Renaissance period in the Western world occurred first in time?

a. Gutenberg's invention of the movable type printing press
b. The end to the Hundred Years' War of England and France
c. The fall of Constantinople and Byzantium to the Ottomans
d. Christopher Columbus's visit to the New World of Americas

14. Which is a true statement about how the Middle Ages gave way to the Renaissance?

a. The change in periods was quite abrupt in historical terms
b. The same events led to this change across various nations
c. The change in the periods was actually a gradual transition
d. The change relates to various time periods among nations

15. After the fall of the Han Dynasty, which dynasty was next to reunite North and South China?

a. The Tang Dynasty
b. The Song Dynasty
c. The Sui Dynasty
d. No dynasty

16. What is true about the golden age in China between the 7th and 13th centuries A.D.?

a. The Chinese had no knowledge of movable type until the 15th century when Gutenberg invented the printing press in Germany
b. The Chinese were not involved with algebra, which was developed by the Arabs; they learned it from them without changes
c. The years during this golden age brought great prosperity and power to China, while its population remained stable
d. The Chinese achieved the innovation of manufacturing gunpowder during this golden age, enabling explosive weaponry

17. Which of the following is accurate about China's golden age between 618 and 1279 A.D.?

a. Toward the end of this age, China strengthened the Silk Road trade routes
b. Importing Vietnamese rice enabled annual harvests to double in this period
c. The later Song Dynasty ruled a larger part of China than the Han or Tang did
d. This period included religious development but not mutual religion exchange

18. Of the following, which Renaissance figure was best known as a fine artist and painter?

a. Dante
b. Petrarch
c. Masaccio
d. Gutenberg

19. Which Italian Renaissance figure was best known as a political philosopher?

a. Dante Alighieri
b. Leonardo Da Vinci
c. Francesco Petrarca
d. Niccolò Machiavelli

20. Which of the following was first to write a work in vernacular Italian rather than Latin?

a. Dante Alighieri
b. Niccolò Machiavelli
c. Francesco Petrarca
d. Pico della Mirandola

21. In Western Europe, which ancient Greek's works would most likely have been studied by scholars before the Renaissance in the Middle Ages?

a. Homer
b. Sophocles
c. Thucydides
d. Archimedes

22. Of the following, whose ancient civilization was found in what is now Peru?

a. The Mayans
b. The Aztecs
c. The Incas
d. All of these

23. Which of these ancient American civilizations was NOT known to have a written language?

a. All of these
b. The Mayans
c. The Aztecs
d. The Incas

24. Which Pre-Columbian American civilization consisted of multiple independent states without a centralized government?

a. The Inca
b. The Maya
c. The Aztec
d. All of these

25. Which of the following world religions believes in many gods and goddesses?

a. Confucianism
b. Hinduism
c. Sikhism
d. Islam

26. Which of these statements is most characteristic of the teachings of Buddhism?

a. There is nothing that is really permanent
b. Everyone has sinned, requiring salvation
c. Living ethically in this life is most valuable
d. Submit to God's will for Paradise at death

27. Regarding Renaissance art, which description is most true?

a. The revival of classic antiquity de-emphasized the natural world
b. The revival of classic antiquity overlooked individual differences
c. The Renaissance paintings were more religious and less realistic
d. The idealization of forms reflected the idea of God's perfection

28. What best represents a key difference of ancient Greek philosophy as reflected in its drama versus modern Western thinking?

a. Punishment was for a deed committed, regardless of intention
b. Ancient Greeks believed in free will rather than predestination
c. In ancient Greek plays, character motivations trumped actions
d. Greek dramatic characters could avert fate through their virtues

29. As a form of government, what does oligarchy mean?

a. Rule by one
b. Rule by a few
c. Rule by law
d. Rule by many

30. What is true about Hammurabi's Code?

a. It predates the concept of innocent until proven guilty
b. It does not address the matter of providing evidence
c. It has been considered as a rudimentary constitution
d. It deals more with domestic rather than contractual matters

31. Which statement is correct regarding the Jewish Ten Commandments?

a. Honoring one's parents is separate from and unrelated to showing respect for God
b. There is no organizational division between the five commandments on each tablet
c. Performing duties to God takes precedence over performing duties to other people
d. If forced to choose between God and people, one must do mitzvoth for people first

32. What is accurate about Emperor Justinian's code, Corpus Juris Civilis (Body of Civil Law)?

a. It is considered to have been the foundation for Western legal tradition
b. It has had much more influence on common-law systems than on civil laws
c. It has been unrelated to the Roman Catholic Church or any of its Canon law
d. It was contradicted by the Napoleonic Code's major modern legal reforms

33. Which of the following is correct regarding the Magna Carta?

a. It exercised an influence upon the subsequent, similar Charter of Liberties
b. It was the first English document to limit monarchic power by the subjects
c. It has not been known to have any relationship with the U.S. Constitution
d. It is considered a very important document but not of constitutional type

34. What was the Neolithic Revolution characterized by?

a. Denser to more spread-out populations
b. More sedentary to more mobile societies
c. Local to central governments and politics
d. More complex to more simplified labor

35. Which scientist first proposed the heliocentric universe instead of a geocentric one?

a. Galileo
b. Ptolemy
c. Copernicus
d. Isaac Newton

36. Which of the following ancient historical events occurred the latest in time?

a. The last of the Punic Wars was ended
b. The Romans began world domination
c. The Mayans produced a new calendar
d. The Chinese first built their Great Wall

37. Which of the following Roman authors lived the earliest in time?

a. Ovid
b. Virgil
c. Cicero
d. Horace

38. Which statement is true about Cleopatra?

a. Cleopatra's union with Julius Caesar produced no offspring
b. Cleopatra and Mark Antony joined forces to oppose Caesar
c. Cleopatra committed suicide, and Mark Antony followed suit
d. Cleopatra was a member of the Greek royal Ptolemy family

39. Which of the following was chronologically the latest action of Roman Emperor Constantine the Great?

a. Issuing the Edict of Milan, legalizing Christianity
b. His conversion to the Christian religion himself
c. Establishing the new capital of Constantinople
d. Being the last to rule a unified Roman Empire

40. Which tribal ruler deposed the last of the Roman emperors in Europe?

a. Attila
b. Clovis
c. Odoacer
d. Theodoric

41. During the early Medieval period in Europe, before the 5th century, where were the main centers of literacy found?

a. They were in the homes of the wealthy
b. They were in the churches and monasteries
c. They were in the local artisan and craft guilds
d. There were no centers of literacy

42. Which of the following is true of the feudal system of organization in Europe?

a. It was first used in France by the Normans
b. It was first used in England by the Saxons
c. It was introduced to France by the English
d. It was a way to centralize the government

43. Which of the following was a common factor related to the falls of both the Western Roman Empire in Europe and the Han Dynasty in China?

a. Strict political ethics
b. Powerful conquerors
c. Government surpluses
d. Survival through religion

44. Of the following, which civilization was NOT an influence on the development of the medieval Byzantine Empire?

a. Greek civilization
b. Roman civilization
c. Eastern civilization
d. All of these

45. Which statement is true about religious developments in medieval Byzantium?

a. Islam overtook Christianity to develop a mainly Islamic civilization in Byzantium
b. Christianity overcame Islam to develop primarily Byzantine culture in Byzantium
c. Islam and Christianity respectively developed Islamic and Byzantine civilizations
d. Conflicts between Islam and Christianity prevented the growth of any civilization

46. What is correct regarding conditions leading up to the Great Schism?

a. There were no major differences within the Catholic Church in the 4th and 5th centuries
b. Differences between Eastern and Western Christianity built up for 700 years
c. Theological differences between East and West contributed but not language difference
d. The Great Schism was caused only by disagreements of the Eastern and Western bishops

47. Which of these was a disagreement about Christian doctrine contributing to the Great Schism?

a. The Eastern Orthodox Church rejected the idea of the Immaculate Conception
b. The Western Roman Catholic Church challenged the infallibility of Rome's Pope
c. The Eastern Orthodox Church was the only one embracing the idea of purgatory
d. The Roman Catholic Church rejected the insertion of "Son" to the Nicene Creed

48. Which of the following events associated with the transition from the Middle Ages to the Renaissance in the Western world was the latest in time?

a. Martin Luther's posting of his 95 Theses at Wittenberg
b. Christopher Columbus's ships landing in the Americas
c. The end to England and France's Hundred Years' War
d. Gutenberg inventing the movable-type printing press

49. Which two consecutive national dynasties were associated with a golden age in China when it led the world in wealth, power, and technology?

a. The Han and Tang Dynasties
b. The Tang and Song Dynasties
c. The Han and Sui Dynasties
d. The Song and Sui Dynasties

50. Which is true of innovations by China during its golden age from the 7th through the 13th centuries A.D.?

a. Porcelain ceramics existed for years before this golden age
b. China imported mechanical clocks made in other countries
c. The production of paper money did not begin until later on
d. China developed magnetic compasses aiding sea navigation

51. What is correct about cultural aspects of China's golden age from 689 to 1279 A.D.?

a. The Song Dynasty was known for Li Bo's poetry
b. The Tang Dynasty was known for Tu Fu's poetry
c. The Tang Dynasty was known for Taoist painting
d. China had foreign trade but no foreign residents

52. Who was best known as a poet of the early European Renaissance?

a. Masaccio
b. Da Vinci
c. Petrarch
d. Donatello

53. Prior to the Renaissance, who studied ancient Greek literature in Europe?

a. Medieval Byzantine scholars
b. Medieval Islamic scholars
c. Medieval Latin scholars
d. No one

54. In Western Europe, ancient Greek texts on which subjects were NOT studied in the Middle Ages but recovered in the Renaissance?

a. Mathematics
b. Philosophy
c. Sciences
d. History

55. Who is least associated with restoring the culture of classical Greek antiquity to Western Europe in the Renaissance, which prepared the way for the Protestant Reformation?

a. Pico della Mirandola
b. Coluccio Salutati
c. Lorenzo Valla
d. Erasmus

56. What is the most accurate statement about Islamic art as reflective of its culture?

a. Calligraphy developed out of reverence for the Qur'an
b. Islamic custom dictates not decorating utilitarian objects
c. Arabic script is not aesthetically appealing for uses in art
d. Art for art's sake is more important than ornamentation

57. The changes from Medieval to Renaissance music featured a shift:

a. From vertical structure to horizontal structure
b. From horizontal structure to vertical structure
c. From harmony using thirds to harmony using fifths
d. From cadences on octaves to cadences on unisons

58. How is a theocracy classified as a form of government?

a. A type of democracy
b. A type of socialism
c. A type of autocracy
d. A type of oligarchy

59. The Code of Hammurabi contains the largest proportion of provisions related to which of the following issues?

a. Grounds for dismissing an official for job performance errors
b. Those arising in conjunction with aspects of military service
c. Relations of paternity, divorce, inheritance, and sexual conduct
d. Property damage or liability for defective products or services

60. Which is correct regarding the Jewish Ten Commandments?

a. There are a great many more commandments in the Jewish Bible
b. There is the same number of commandments in the Jewish Bible
c. The Ten Commandments are based on the Bible commandments
d. There are no additional commandments in the Bible, only the Ten

Answers and Explanations

1. A: The first centralized governments were developed concurrently and independently by the ancient river valley civilizations about 5,000 years ago, that is, from around 3000 to 2000 B.C. These societies included the Egyptian, Nubian, and Mesopotamian civilizations in the Middle East; the Harappan civilization in India; and China's Yellow River valley civilizations. In ancient Greece, Plato recorded Socrates's Dialogues between 400 and 300 B.C., and the Parthenon was built around the 400s B.C. The Torah, or first five books of the Old Testament, was recorded in Aramaic by the Jews between 400 and 300 B.C.

2. B: Ancient Greek physician Hippocrates, known as the "Father of Medicine" and after whom the Hippocratic Oath still used today was named, lived circa 460 to 370 B.C. before mathematician Euclid developed his system of geometry and also before scientist Archimedes discovered the principle of displacement of water by solid objects while taking a bath, both in the 200s B.C. The Temple of the Sun was constructed at Teotihuacán, Mexico, circa 300 B.C., after Hippocrates's death. Ancient Greek philosopher Aristotle (384–322 B.C.), first to produce a comprehensive Western philosophical system, produced the bulk of his work between 335 and 323 B.C., after Hippocrates's lifetime.

3. C: The Jewish rebel army of the Maccabees staged an uprising against the Seleucid Empire in 167 B.C. This rebellion was notable as the Maccabees reestablished Jewish control of Judea, reaffirmed the Jewish religion, extended Israel's boundaries, and founded the Hasmonean Dynasty (164–63 B.C.), which some historians believe set the Jewish Biblical canon. A number of rebellions against the Roman Republic were made by its slaves, the most notable one led by the slave Spartacus in 71 B.C. Roman Emperor Julius Caesar, instrumental in turning the Roman Republic into the Roman Empire, was assassinated as a dictator through a conspiracy by a group of his senators in 44 B.C. Cleopatra ruled Egypt from 51 B.C. until her 30 B.C. suicide.

4. D: The Council of Nicaea first outlined the doctrines of Orthodox Christianity in 325 A.D. This occurred after Emperor Constantine the Great issued the Edict of Milan legalizing Christianity in 313. The increasing invasions of Gothic and Frankish tribes in Europe took place in the second half of the 3rd century A.D., that is, circa 250–300. Roughly 30 years after the Romans crucified Jesus Christ, they initiated more widespread persecution of Christians in 64 A.D. (This persecution intensified even more in the 200s, but the tribal invasions combined with inadequate leadership undermined the Western Roman Empire, contributing to the fall of the Roman Empire and allowing Christianity to spread in the absence of Rome's unifying power.)

5. D: The foundation of the Kingdom of Italy by Visigoth (East German tribal ancestor) Theodoric the Great took place in 493 A.D. King Alaric I had previously sacked the city of Rome in the year 410 A.D., the first time Rome had fallen to an enemy in 800 years. In 433 A.D., Attila the Hun, a chieftain of the Mongol tribes from central Asia, attacked a number of provinces that Rome had ruled. The Vandals, an Eastern Germanic tribe, destroyed the city of Rome in 455 A.D. Theodoric established the Kingdom of Italy 38 years later.

6. C: In Europe, the Middle Ages, or Medieval period, lasted from approximately 500 to 1500 A.D. It began with the fall of the Western Roman Empire and ended with the beginning of the Renaissance (meaning rebirth), when interest in knowledge and culture were reawakened, including a revival of the ancient Greek and Roman influences from before the Middle Ages.

7. B: In 1079, Pope Gregory VII issued a papal decree that mandated the establishment of cathedral schools to educate the clergy. This resulted in multiple educational centers, which eventually developed into medieval universities. Charlemagne, the King of the Carolingian Empire, reigned earlier, during the 9th century. He was responsible for decreeing the creation of the earlier cathedral schools to educate boys to become clerical bureaucrats for the administration of the Empire. Robert Sorbon sponsored a theological college in Paris, France, later than Pope Gregory's 1079 decree, in 1231; it developed over centuries into Sorbonne University. John Balliol founded one of the earliest colleges, Balliol College in Oxford, England, in 1260.

8. A: In both the Han Dynasty of China and the Western Roman Empire of Europe, the populations were reduced by epidemics of plagues. Both did not reign for the same duration: The Han Dynasty lasted around 200 years, while the Western Roman Empire lasted around 900 years. Both were not succeeded by stronger empires; both empires fell not to stronger rulers or regimes but to multiple damages, including the plagues, low birth rates, conflicts and political corruption from within, and barbarian tribes' invasions from without. An additional factor was the influence of income taxes: Both empires failed to collect sufficient tax monies to support their governments.

9. A: It is true that, in the Medieval period, Byzantium continued for 1,100 years beyond the foundation of the capital of Constantinople in 330 A.D. Byzantium was the name for the Christian part of the Eastern Roman Empire. Hence, it was primarily Christian in religion until the 7th century, preserving Mediterranean Roman culture until Islam began to develop in Eastern Europe. Medieval Byzantium was not unstable but was the most stable European state during those times. Byzantium's strongest times were noted not for intellectual advances but for religious development.

10. B: The Eastern European state of Byzantium in the Middle Ages helped to prepare the way for the emergence of the Renaissance in Europe through Byzantine ethnic diversity, stability, cultural strength, its central location, world prominence, urban centers comprising a network, and multiple cultural influences. These factors encouraged rather than delayed the Renaissance. Byzantium was unified and stable but not antithetical to coming Renaissance diversity; Byzantium too was characterized by diversity, among the ethnicity of its populations and cultural influences from Greek, Roman, and Oriental civilizations.

11. C: In the early days of Christianity in Europe, the Western Christian Church was governed by one bishop situated in Rome. However, the Eastern Christian Church was governed by multiple bishops at locations including Antioch, Jerusalem, Alexandria, and Constantinople. The government of the Roman Empire did recognize Christianity and by the 4th, not 5th, century: Emperor Constantine the Great legalized Christianity in 313 A.D. through the Edict of Milan. In fact, by the 5th century, Christianity was the only religion recognized by Roman government. Even in the 4th century, though, Eastern and Western Europe's Christianity differed, not only politically but also socially, culturally, and linguistically: The Western Church spoke Latin, but the Eastern Church spoke Greek.

12. D: The Great Schism permanently divided the Catholic Church into the Roman Catholic Church in Western Europe and the Eastern Orthodox Church in Eastern Europe. This occurred during the 11th century A.D. and not the 10th. It did not involve Protestants, who did not emerge until the 16th century with the Protestant Reformation spearheaded by Martin Luther. It did not separate Christianity from other religions but was an internal splitting of the Catholic Church.

13. A: Gutenberg invented the movable-type printing press in 1445. This replaced handwriting for the mass production of books, enabling a shift from medieval public illiteracy to mass literacy that contributed to the Renaissance explosion of revived interest in education and culture. The Hundred Years' War between England and France ended in 1453. Consequently, England moved from continental power to naval strength; and the nations of Europe began to develop modern militaries and political states. Also in 1453, the Ottomans took Constantinople, signaling the end of the Byzantine Empire and beginning of the Ottoman Empire in Eastern Europe. Columbus landed in Central America in 1492 and subsequently explored the Americas, marking the start of European colonial expansion abroad.

14. C: The change from the Medieval to the Renaissance time period did not occur suddenly but happened through a gradual transitional process. This transition was stimulated by different events in different nations. It also occurred during different time periods within the longer timeline in different countries. Because of these factors, historians rightly avoid assigning specific dates or events to the end of the Middle Ages and the beginning of the Renaissance.

15. B: The Song Dynasty reunited North and South China. China's Han Dynasty fell in 220 A.D. There followed many local dynasties for 350 years, but none was able to reunite China. In 589 A.D., the Emperor Wendi achieved reunification of the Northern and Southern parts of the country with the Sui Dynasty. During the Sui years, the Grand Canal was built and the Great Wall of China rebuilt. However, despite these achievements, peasants rebelled against the associated labor and taxation, overthrowing the Sui by 618. It was succeeded by the Tang Dynasty, which reigned from 618 to 907. At the end of the Tang, China was decentralized until 960, when General Taizu reunited it, becoming the first emperor of the Song Dynasty.

16. D: One of many innovations during China's golden age from 618 to 1279 under the Tang and Song Dynasties was the development of gunpowder, an advance benefiting the military by allowing explosives manufacture. Although Gutenberg invented Europe's first movable-type printing press in 1445 in Renaissance Germany, the Chinese also invented movable-type printing earlier in their country during this golden age, while Europe was still in the Middle Ages, isolated without the Roman Empire's previous knowledge, culture, and trade connections, so this Chinese innovation did not spread to Europe then. The Arabs did develop algebra; however, the Chinese also added innovations to both algebra and arithmetic, including negative numbers, during this golden age. This period brought not only wealth and power; China's population also doubled.

17. B: During China's golden age between the 7th and 13th centuries A.D., an agricultural innovatin was its importation of a strain of Vietnamese rice that ripened faster, enabling farmers to reap double the annual crops to feed the rapidly growing populations of China's cities. While earlier in the Tang Dynasty, its imperial guards protected the east–west trade routes of the Silk Roads, later on as the dynasty gradually declined, it lost control of these overland routes. The Chinese invention of the magnetic compass helped them transition to maritime trading. The Song Dynasty actually ruled a smaller empire than the Han or Tang Dynasty. However, the Song did perpetuate the power, wealth, and stability of China established during the Tang period. China's golden age did include mutual exchange of religions: Vietnam, Korea, and Japan learned of Buddhism from China, while Eastern Orthodox Christianity and Islam were introduced to China through trade with Europe and the Middle East.

18. C: Masaccio was an Italian fine artist and painter of the Renaissance. He was known for being the first to use linear perspective and the vanishing point in his paintings. He also used chiaroscuro (a technique of contrasting light and dark). His paintings were innovative for being more realistic, three-dimensional, and lifelike. Dante (Alighieri), also Italian, was a writer most famous for his Divine Comedy as well as La Vita Nuova (The New Life) and other works. Petrarch was another Italian and was a great lyrical poet of the Renaissance. Gutenberg, a German, was famous for inventing a movable-type printing press during the Renaissance.

19. D: Niccolò Machiavelli, perhaps best known for his book *The Prince*, was an Italian Renaissance political philosopher noted for writing more realistic representations and rational interpretations of politics. In *The Prince*, he popularized the political concept of "the ends justify the means." Dante Alighieri was a great poet famous for his *Commedia* (additionally labeled *Divina* by contemporary poet and author Boccaccio, who wrote *The Decameron* and other works) or *Divine Comedy*, a trilogy consisting of *Inferno*, *Purgatorio*, and *Paradiso* (*Hell*, *Purgatory*, and *Heaven*). Dante's work helped propel the transition from the Medieval period to the Renaissance. Francesco Petrarca, known in English as Petrarch, was famous for his lyrical poetry, particularly sonnets.

20. A: Dante Alighieri wrote his Divine Comedy, the first major literary work known to be written in Italian, between 1308 and 1321. In the Medieval period, the masses were illiterate, and the only reading and writing was done by religious scholars in Latin, the language of the Roman Empire. Vernacular languages subsequently developed in Europe when Latin mixed with local languages and evolved into Italian, French, Spanish, and so on. Machiavelli wrote his most famous book, Il Principe (The Prince), and other works in Italian but in the 16th century, 200 years after Dante. Francesco Petrarca, or Petrarch, lived and wrote in the 14th century. He wrote some poetry in Italian, but as a scholar and fan of Latin, he wrote other poetry and many other works mostly in Latin. Pico della Mirandola, a Renaissance humanist famous for his 1486 oration De Hominis Dignitate (On the Dignity of Man), wrote this and his other works in Latin.

21. D: Archimedes was an ancient Greek physicist, mathematician, astronomer, engineer, and inventor. He made many innovations, especially in physics. During the Middle Ages, Western European scholars did study ancient Greek texts but only those pertaining to mathematics, the sciences, and philosophy and theology. They did not study ancient Greek works of poetry, drama, oratory, or history. Homer was an ancient Greek poet, Sophocles an ancient Greek dramatist, and Thucydides an ancient Greek historian. Until the Renaissance, only Byzantine scholars in Eastern Europe studied these works.

22. C: The ancient civilization of the Incas was located in what is today the South American country of Peru. The ancient civilization of the Mayans lived in the south of Mexico, on the Yucatan peninsula, and in parts of Central America. The ancient civilization of the Aztecs lived in what is Mexico today.

23. D: The Incas, as far as historians know, did NOT commit their spoken language to a written symbol system. (Note that some historians believe that strings the Incas knotted, called Quipu, may have equated to a writing system, though this has not been verified.) The Mayans were known for developing the most comprehensive, authentic written language of the Pre-Columbian Native American societies. A play written in Achi, one of the Mayan languages, has been deemed a masterpiece by the United Nations Educational, Scientific and Cultural Organization (UNESCO). The Aztecs' written language was Nàhuatl.

24. B: The ancient Mayan civilization was the only one of these three that consisted of many independent states spread over a territory including today's Central American countries of Honduras, Belize, and El Salvador; the Yucatan peninsula; and the south of Mexico. The Incas in today's Peru in South America and the Aztecs in today's Mexico were both societies with centralized governments that were more easily vanquished by Spain's conquistadores. The Maya resisted domination much longer, and their peoples survived in part due to their decentralization.

25. B: Followers of Hinduism, an indigenous religion of India, believes in one Supreme Reality (Brahman), manifested in many different gods and goddesses that oversee different aspects of life. Confucianism, a Chinese religion, does not address whether there are many gods or one. Followers of Sikhism, an Indian religion originating in Punjab, believe in a single god, Om or Ik Om Kar. Islam, founded by Muhammad in Saudi Arabia, purports a single god, Allah.

26. A: The Buddha taught that nothing is permanent. Gaining enlightenment would release one from the cycle of rebirth; attaining merit through one's life would at least bring a better rebirth. The statement that everyone has sinned and must seek salvation is most characteristic of Christianity. The statement that living ethically in this life is most valuable—that is, more important than the afterlife—is characteristic of Judaism as well as Christianity and Islam. Living ethically at its most basic level meant obeying God's commandments. The statement that submitting to the will of God (Allah) would bring one to Paradise after dying is most typical of Islam.

27. D: A key feature of the Renaissance was the revival of the classical works of ancient Greek and Roman civilizations. Renaissance humanism reflected classical ideals: Artists emphasized the natural world and individual differences as classical artists had. Medieval paintings were mainly religious and not realistic; in the Renaissance, artists strove for more realistic, naturalistic representations of life. Italian Renaissance artists particularly reflected ideals of classical art in that both idealized human bodies and other forms, such as architecture, as a spiritual practice to mirror the perfection of God.

28. A: A key difference between ancient Greek philosophy, as seen in dramatic works, and modern Western thought is that the deed committed dictated its punishment regardless of the doer's intentions. For example, in Sophocles's tragedy Oedipus Rex (Oedipus the King), Oedipus unknowingly kills his father and marries his mother; the fact that he did not do these things intentionally or even knowingly does not matter; he is just as guilty regardless of motivation. In modern Western thinking, one's intentions determine the offense: In American law, premeditated murder carries more serious punishment than involuntary manslaughter. Oedipus Rex also demonstrates the ancient Greek belief in predestination over free will: Oedipus is predestined to commit these acts as the Oracle of Delphi predicted, regardless of all efforts to prevent them. This play clearly shows the belief that nothing could be done to avert fate.

29. B: Oligarchy is defined as the rule by few. An example is aristocracy, which in ancient Greece, was government by an elite group of citizens as opposed to a monarchy. In later times, it meant government by the class of aristocrats, a privileged group, as opposed to democracy. The rule of one is called autocracy. Examples include monarchy, dictatorship, and many others. The rule by law is called a republic. Some examples are constitutional republics, parliamentary republics, and federal republics. The rule by many could apply to democracy, which governs according to the people's votes or to the collective leadership form of socialism, where no one individual has too much power.

30. C: The Babylonian king Hammurabi wrote his Code circa 1700 B.C. It is considered by some to represent an early example of a basic form of constitution. It is also significant as one of the earliest expressions of the concept that one is innocent until proven guilty, which it did not predate. Hammurabi's Code also addresses the matter of providing evidence, suggesting that both a citizen accusing another and the accused have the right to supply evidence on their own behalf's. There are more provisions in Hammurabi's Code addressing contractual matters—for example, determining wages for given services and liability in transactions, and so on (these make up nearly half of the Code)—than provisions for domestic matters, for example, inheritance, paternity, divorce, and so on, which make up roughly one third of the Code.

31. D: According to Jewish rabbinical teachings, the five Commandments on the left side of the tablet concern a person's relationship with God, and the five on the right side concern a person's relationship with other people. The Commandment to honor one's parents is on the left side because parents create the child, so their relationship mirrors that of God creating humans as His children. Hence disrespect to parents is an insult to God. The rabbis also teach that both sides of the Commandments are parallel, that is, equal. Duties to God and to other people are considered equally important. If, however, one is forced to choose, he or she should perform good deeds (mitzvoth) for other people before performing duties for God.

32. A: The set of laws developed by Eastern Roman Emperor Justinian, which he issued from 529 to 534 A.D., is generally regarded as the basis for the Western legal tradition. While Justinian's "code" had little influence on common-law systems, it eventually became the basis for all civil law. Justinian's code also had a strong influence on the Canon law of the Roman Catholic Church. It established Christianity as the official religion of the Roman Empire; non-Christians or those not associated with the Catholic Church were deemed noncitizens. The biggest legal reform of the modern era—the Napoleonic Code, which did away with the medieval feudal system—was also based on the legal philosophy of Justinian's code.

33. B: The Magna Carta (1215) was the first English document wherein a king's powers were limited and the rights of his subjects protected and the first time subjects (feudal barons) forced the king to accept such an agreement. At the time, it applied to King John. The Magna Carta did not influence the Charter of Liberties, which was not subsequent: The Charter of Liberties, issued in 1100, influenced the Magna Carta. The Magna Carta also had an influence on the United States Constitution. The Magna Carta is not only considered a document of vital importance but is, moreover, considered a constitutional document. Judge and King's Counsel Lord Denning (1899–1999) described it as "the greatest constitutional document of all times."

34. C: The Neolithic Revolution (c. 8000–5000 B.C.) was the beginning of agriculture, with plants and animals being domesticated in several locations worldwide. Civilizations shifted from hunting and gathering to planting crops and raising animals. This resulted in greater population densities as villages and towns developed. Societies changed from mobile groups that followed food sources to sedentary settlements cultivating foods and stockpiling surpluses. Government administrations and political systems became centralized and hierarchical. Labor evolved from simpler to more complex and diversified, and economies of trade developed.

35. C: Copernicus's *De revolutionibus orbium coelestium* (On the Revolutions of the Heavenly Spheres) was published in 1543, almost simultaneously with his death. He was the first to contradict the then-accepted belief that the Earth was the center of the universe and the Sun and other bodies moved around it. This geocentric model was associated with Ptolemy and hence called the Ptolemaic system. Galileo Galilei published Siderius Nuncius (Starry Messenger) in 1610. In it, he revealed his observations, made through his improvements to the telescope, which corroborated Copernicus's theory. Sir Isaac Newton (1642–1727) built the first usable reflecting telescope and erased any lingering doubts about a heliocentric universe by describing universal gravitation and showing its congruence with Kepler's laws of planetary motion.

36. A: The First Punic War began in 264 B.C. In the Third, and last, Punic War, the Romans completely destroyed Carthage, ending all vestiges of the Carthaginian Empire in 146 B.C. The Romans' world dominion had begun with their defeat of Seleucid King Antiochus III at the Battle of Thermopylae in 191 B.C. The Mayans produced a new, more accurate calendar circa 300 B.C. The Chinese first constructed the Great Wall of China circa 215 B.C. Hence 146 B.C., the end of the last Punic War, was the event latest in time.

37. C: Famous Roman orator, statesman, and political and philosophical writer Cicero, who introduced the Romans to Greek philosophy and humanism, lived from 106 to 43 B.C. Roman poet Ovid, known for his Metamorphoses, lived from 43 B.C. to 14 A.D. Roman poet Virgil, known for his Aeneid, lived from 70 to 19 B.C. Horace, the Roman satirist and lyric poet, lived from 65 to 8 B.C.

38. D: Cleopatra was a member of the Ptolemaic Dynasty, a Greek royal family who ruled Egypt during the Hellenistic Period after the death of Alexander the Great. Her union with Julius Caesar, which she arranged to reinforce her role as ruler, did produce a child, Caesarion, whom she later named as her co-ruler. His supporters named him Pharaoh briefly following Cleopatra's death, but he was then killed by Octavian (later called Caesar Augustus), Julius Caesar's heir and successor. Cleopatra joined with Mark Antony against Octavian, not against Julius Caesar, after Julius Caesar's assassination. Mark Antony committed suicide, and Cleopatra followed suit, not vice versa. (She had ordered her servants to tell him she was dead; believing this on top of being defeated by Octavian, Antony stabbed himself. Cleopatra saw him before he died; upon his death, she arranged her own suicide.)

39. B: Emperor Constantine the Great did much to further Christianity, such as issuing the Edict of Milan in 313 A.D. to legalize Christianity, but he only converted to the religion himself upon his deathbed in 337 A.D. Constantine established a new Eastern capital of the Roman Empire in 330 A.D. in present-day Istanbul, named Constantinople after him at the time, upon the site of the former Byzantium. Constantine achieved a temporary reunification of the Eastern and Western parts of the Roman Empire. He was, however, not the last to rule a unified Roman Empire; Theodosius the Great was. By 395 A.D., the Roman Empire had permanently divided into Eastern and Western Empires.

40. C: Odoacer's deposition of Romulus Augustulus, the last Roman Emperor, to become King of Italy in 476 is considered by historians as the ending of the Western Roman Empire. Attila the Hun and his "Mongol hordes" attacked Roman territories earlier in the 5th century. Clovis was a king of the Frankish tribe and ruled areas that are now France; he also converted to Christianity in 496, influencing public adoption of the religion. Theodoric the Great, an Ostrogoth (Eastern German tribal) king, was Odoacer's successor and established the Kingdom of Italy in place of Roman rule circa 496.

41. B: During the early Medieval period (or Middle Ages), Europe was characterized by widespread illiteracy, ignorance, and superstition once the unifying influence of the Roman Empire was lost. Few universities, like the university at Constantinople founded in 2 A.D. and those at Athens, Antioch, and Alexandria around the same time, existed then. Before the 5th and 6th centuries A.D., any education was conducted at cathedral or monastery schools or privately in the homes of wealthy families, which cannot be considered "main centers of literacy." More religious schools were created through Charlemagne's reforms in the 9th century, and early forms of universities began developing in the 11th and 12th centuries.

42. A: The Normans, a tribe associated with Normandy in France, began using the feudal system around 900 A.D. It was not until the Norman invasion of England in 1066 by William the Conqueror, who deposed the last Saxon (a Germanic tribal ancestor of English, Dutch, and ethnic German peoples) king, that feudalism was introduced to England. Thereafter, it spread widely throughout Western Europe. Feudal systems typically developed where governments were not centralized as local alternatives. Feudalism only receded when strong, central monarchies were established in various European nations.

43. D: In China, religion helped people survive following the fall of the Han Dynasty; religion also helped Eastern Europeans to endure following the fall of the Western Roman Empire. Political corruption contributed to the falls of both empires rather than strict ethics. Neither of these empires fell to powerful conquerors but to multiple damages, including from corrupt politics; diseases; attacks by barbarian tribes; and government funding shortages, not surpluses, due to inadequate tax collections.

44. D: The medieval Byzantine Empire in Eastern Europe was influenced by all three civilizations: The Alexandrian/Hellenic civilization of the Greeks was native to the Mediterranean region; the Romans' subsequent conquest of the Greeks and other European civilizations contributed their widespread cultural influence; and influences from Eastern or Oriental civilizations were brought through trade, travel, and Byzantium's central location and major position as a world culture.

45. C: Medieval Byzantium incorporated influences from both Islam and Christianity. Due to inherent differences between the two religions, Islamic civilization was developed through Muslim influences, while Byzantine civilization was developed through Christian influences. Neither religion overtook the other to develop one primary culture in Byzantium. Due to its size, ethnic diversity, and multiple cultural influences, civilization grew in medieval Byzantium and was not prevented by conflicts between the religions.

46. B: Even when Christianity was first legalized in the Roman Empire by Constantine in 313 A.D., and even when it was the only religion recognized by Roman rule by the 5th century, major differences existed between the Eastern and Western Christian Churches. These built up over 700 years, leading to the 11th century's Great Schism in the Catholic Church of Europe. The differences were theological, political, social, cultural, and linguistic—the Eastern Church spoke Greek, while the Western Church spoke Latin. The Schism's causes were these multiple differences and not disagreements of bishops. In fact, one political difference was that the Western Church was led by one bishop in Rome, while the Eastern Church was governed by multiple bishops in different cities.

47. A: In addition to differences in language, culture, society, and politics, differences in theology contributed to the Great Schism dividing the Catholic Church into Roman Catholic and Eastern Orthodox Churches in the 11th century. Among these, the Eastern Orthodox Church rejected the doctrine of the Virgin Mary's Immaculate Conception of Jesus Christ, in which the Western Roman Catholic Church believed. The Roman Catholic Church also subscribed to the Roman Pope's infallibility regarding Church doctrine, but the Eastern Orthodox did not. Eastern Orthodox Christians also rejected the concept of purgatory, which was embraced by the Western Roman Catholics. Moreover, Roman Catholicism inserted "... and the Son" (after God) to the eighth article of the Nicene Creed, which established Christian doctrines, but the Eastern Orthodox objected to this addition as unauthorized.

48. A: Martin Luther posted his 95 Theses on the door of the cathedral at Wittenberg in 1517, outlining his reasons for breaking away from the Catholic Church. This reduced the power of Catholicism over Europe, allowing the intellectual inquiry and diversity of the Renaissance. Columbus landed in the Americas in 1492, signaling the onset of European exploration and expansionism to other continents, which was compatible with Renaissance ideas. The Hundred Years' War between England and France ended in 1453. Thereafter England refocused its former continental domination to develop great naval forces, and European nations began creating more modern states and armies. Gutenberg's printing press invention in 1445 allowed mass publishing, enabling the public to become literate again after medieval illiteracy.

49. B: The Tang and Song Dynasties were separated by 53 years, but during those interim years, only local dynasties ruled, and there was no national unity. Thus, the Tang and Song were consecutive national dynasties in China. These two dynastic periods created a golden age wherein China became the richest, most powerful, and most technologically advanced country in the world. The Han Dynasty fell in 220 A.D., while the Tang began in 618, so they were nowhere near consecutive. The Sui Dynasty followed the Han chronologically but did not begin until 581—361 years after the Han fell—and the Sui, while responsible for major public accomplishments, only lasted 37 years before being overthrown by peasants. The Song Dynasty ruled from 960 to 1279, while the Sui ruled much earlier, from 581 to 618—not consecutive in either order.

50. D: The Chinese did develop the magnetic compass during its golden age under the Tang and Song Dynasties, which improved nautical navigation, allowing more sea trade. During this golden age, the Chinese developed porcelain (a very fine ceramic made from kaolin, a very pure clay), which did not exist previously. The Chinese also developed mechanical clocks, rather than importing them from other countries, during this period of growth. This time period also did include the Chinese innovation of producing paper money.

51. B: Tu Fu was a great poet during the Tang Dynasty's reign in China. Li Bo was another great poet, also during the Tang Dynasty and not the Song. Exquisite paintings showing Taoist influences were created in China during the later Song Dynasty rather than the earlier Tang period. During the golden age encompassing both the Tang and Song Dynasties' reigns, China not only engaged in much foreign trade, but it also hosted many foreign residents as Arab and other traders came there for commerce and stayed to live in China's flourishing cities.

52. C: Petrarch was an Italian best known for his lyrical poetry, particularly sonnets, as well as being a scholar. He was also one of the first humanists and originated the idea of the "Dark Ages" to describe the Middle Ages before the Renaissance. Masaccio and Donatello were both famous as Italian Renaissance painters. Leonardo Da Vinci was a polymath with many talents, but he was known more for his drawings, paintings, sculptures, architecture, scientific inventions, and so on. He was also a mathematician, engineer, botanist, geologist, anatomist, cartographer, and writer but was not known as a poet.

53. A: In the Middle Ages, only Byzantine scholars studied literary works by the ancient Greeks. Medieval Islamic and Latin scholars studied ancient Greek texts but only those devoted to mathematics, sciences, philosophy, and theology. Greek works of drama, poetry, oratory, and history were only studied by medieval Byzantine scholars. It was not until the Renaissance that Latin and Islamic scholars in Western Europe regained access to the literary works of ancient Greece, creating a Greek revival and contributing to Renaissance Humanism.

54. D: History was one subject within ancient Greek texts that Western Europe's Latin and Islamic scholars did not study during the Middle Ages, when most of the knowledge and culture of ancient Greece and Rome was lost there. Poetry and dramatic and oratorical works were also not studied by Western European scholars in the Middle Ages. In medieval times, these scholars only studied ancient Greek texts covering mathematics, the sciences, philosophy, and theology. Only the Byzantine scholars of Eastern Europe studied ancient Greek literary and historical texts during the Middle Ages. Western European scholars in the Renaissance first recovered ancient Latin works, and then ancient Greek works, and studied them, informing the Renaissance Humanist movement.

55. A: Giovanni Pico della Mirandola's On the Dignity of Man was considered the "Renaissance Manifesto" and a vital contribution to Renaissance Humanism. However, della Mirandola's thinking was eventually influenced by anti-Humanist Savonarola. While well educated in Greek, Aramaic, and Hebrew, as well as Latin, as he believed any good Biblical scholar should be, della Mirandola was not as closely associated with the revival of ancient Greek culture that prepared Europe for the Protestant Reformation as the others: Renaissance scholar Coluccio Salutati invited Manuel Chrysoloras, a Byzantine scholar and diplomat, to come teach Greek in Florence, Italy, prompting a movement to reintegrate ancient Greek literary and historical works into Western European curricula. Lorenzo Valla and Erasmus were both Catholic priests and Renaissance Humanists. Italian educator Valla improved Latin style, restoring it to more classical forms and was admired by Martin Luther who started the Protestant Reformation. Erasmus a Dutch scholar prepared new Greek and Latin versions of the New Testament informed by the original Greek New Testament, raising issues influencing the Protestant Reformation.

56. A: The art of calligraphy was developed early in Islamic cultures because the Qur'an, the Muslim Holy Scripture, was a written document, and the Arabic language unites all Muslims. Muslim artists sought to demonstrate their reverence and love for the Qur'an in their works, so they incorporated the writing using the decorative script of calligraphy. The Arabic script has a unique, aesthetically appealing look very well adapted to artistic uses. Islamic custom also dictates the decoration of utilitarian objects; for example, an ordinary glass bottle holding kohl will be encased in a cloth pouch decorated with embroidery and coins because, in Islam, the Prophet said that "God is beautiful and loves beauty" and "God likes that, when you do anything, you do it excellently." In Islam, ornamentation takes precedence over art for art's sake.

57. B: Medieval tuning and polyphonic music were based on the Pythagorean system and differed from later music. The earliest music in the Middle Ages, the plain chant of Christian monks, had single melody lines with no harmony. This is a horizontal structure as each note moves laterally to the next. Vertical structure is music with chords, where multiple notes are sounded at once as well as having the melody's horizontal movement. The earliest medieval harmonies emphasized octaves and fifths and were called organum. Early music cadences (the closures of individual music phrases) were on unisons (all singing or playing the same note), then cadences on octaves and fifths developed. Later, this changed to triads (thirds) being more harmonically popular. By the High Renaissance, harmonies and cadences were fully based on thirds. This triadic system was a precursor to today's common practice harmony.

58. C: Autocracy is the rule of one. A theocracy is government by one person who is considered to have divine right and divine guidance, or government according to the tenets of a given religion but still by one ruler. Democracy is government according to the will of the people. Socialism is cooperative government (at least in theory) with a philosophy and economic system wherein the means of production is commonly owned or state-owned. Oligarchy is the rule by few, as in the aristocracies of ancient Greece (an elite group of the best citizens) and later in Europe (the privileged aristocratic class).

59. D: Almost half of the provisions of the Code of Hammurabi, written by the Babylonian king circa 1700 B.C., deal with issues related to contracts, such as damage to property while under another's care; liability, such as of a builder for a defective house; or what wages should be paid to various service providers like doctors or laborers. This Code has only one provision related to grounds for dismissing an official for performance errors; it dictates that a judge who makes an incorrect decision be fined and permanently removed from the bench. Issues related to military service are addressed in only a few provisions of the Code. Roughly one third of the Code's provisions address domestic or familial relationships involving a child's paternity, divorces, inheritances, and sexual conduct.

60. A: In the Jewish Bible, there are 613 commandments known as mitzvoth (good deeds), many more than in the actual Ten Commandments. These 613 commandments are ideologically based upon the Jewish Ten Commandments and not vice versa. The "short form" of the Ten Commandments gives the basic tenets of the Jewish code of moral behavior. The 613 commandments given in the Bible's mitzvoth are much more detailed, pertaining to more specific aspects of moral and ethical behavior in life

How to Overcome Test Anxiety

Just the thought of taking a test is enough to make most people a little nervous. A test is an important event that can have a long-term impact on your future, so it's important to take it seriously and it's natural to feel anxious about performing well. But just because anxiety is normal, that doesn't mean that it's helpful in test taking, or that you should simply accept it as part of your life. Anxiety can have a variety of effects. These effects can be mild, like making you feel slightly nervous, or severe, like blocking your ability to focus or remember even a simple detail.

If you experience test anxiety—whether severe or mild—it's important to know how to beat it. To discover this, first you need to understand what causes test anxiety.

Causes of Test Anxiety

While we often think of anxiety as an uncontrollable emotional state, it can actually be caused by simple, practical things. One of the most common causes of test anxiety is that a person does not feel adequately prepared for their test. This feeling can be the result of many different issues such as poor study habits or lack of organization, but the most common culprit is time management. Starting to study too late, failing to organize your study time to cover all of the material, or being distracted while you study will mean that you're not well prepared for the test. This may lead to cramming the night before, which will cause you to be physically and mentally exhausted for the test. Poor time management also contributes to feelings of stress, fear, and hopelessness as you realize you are not well prepared but don't know what to do about it.

Other times, test anxiety is not related to your preparation for the test but comes from unresolved fear. This may be a past failure on a test, or poor performance on tests in general. It may come from comparing yourself to others who seem to be performing better or from the stress of living up to expectations. Anxiety may be driven by fears of the future—how failure on this test would affect your educational and career goals. These fears are often completely irrational, but they can still negatively impact your test performance.

Elements of Test Anxiety

As mentioned earlier, test anxiety is considered to be an emotional state, but it has physical and mental components as well. Sometimes you may not even realize that you are suffering from test anxiety until you notice the physical symptoms. These can include trembling hands, rapid heartbeat, sweating, nausea, and tense muscles. Extreme anxiety may lead to fainting or vomiting. Obviously, any of these symptoms can have a negative impact on testing. It is important to recognize them as soon as they begin to occur so that you can address the problem before it damages your performance.

The mental components of test anxiety include trouble focusing and inability to remember learned information. During a test, your mind is on high alert, which can help you recall information and stay focused for an extended period of time. However, anxiety interferes with your mind's natural processes, causing you to blank out, even on the questions you know well. The strain of testing during anxiety makes it difficult to stay focused, especially on a test that may take several hours. Extreme anxiety can take a huge mental toll, making it difficult not only to recall test information but even to understand the test questions or pull your thoughts together.

Effects of Test Anxiety

Test anxiety is like a disease—if left untreated, it will get progressively worse. Anxiety leads to poor performance, and this reinforces the feelings of fear and failure, which in turn lead to poor performances on subsequent tests. It can grow from a mild nervousness to a crippling condition. If allowed to progress, test anxiety can have a big impact on your schooling, and consequently on your future.

Test anxiety can spread to other parts of your life. Anxiety on tests can become anxiety in any stressful situation, and blanking on a test can turn into panicking in a job situation. But fortunately, you don't have to let anxiety rule your testing and determine your grades. There are a number of relatively simple steps you can take to move past anxiety and function normally on a test and in the rest of life.

Physical Steps for Beating Test Anxiety

While test anxiety is a serious problem, the good news is that it can be overcome. It doesn't have to control your ability to think and remember information. While it may take time, you can begin taking steps today to beat anxiety.

Just as your first hint that you may be struggling with anxiety comes from the physical symptoms, the first step to treating it is also physical. Rest is crucial for having a clear, strong mind. If you are tired, it is much easier to give in to anxiety. But if you establish good sleep habits, your body and mind will be ready to perform optimally, without the strain of exhaustion. Additionally, sleeping well helps you to retain information better, so you're more likely to recall the answers when you see the test questions.

Getting good sleep means more than going to bed on time. It's important to allow your brain time to relax. Take study breaks from time to time so it doesn't get overworked, and don't study right before bed. Take time to rest your mind before trying to rest your body, or you may find it difficult to fall asleep.

Along with sleep, other aspects of physical health are important in preparing for a test. Good nutrition is vital for good brain function. Sugary foods and drinks may give a burst of energy but this burst is followed by a crash, both physically and emotionally. Instead, fuel your body with protein and vitamin-rich foods.

Also, drink plenty of water. Dehydration can lead to headaches and exhaustion, especially if your brain is already under stress from the rigors of the test. Particularly if your test is a long one, drink water during the breaks. And if possible, take an energy-boosting snack to eat between sections.

Along with sleep and diet, a third important part of physical health is exercise. Maintaining a steady workout schedule is helpful, but even taking 5-minute study breaks to walk can help get your blood pumping faster and clear your head. Exercise also releases endorphins, which contribute to a positive feeling and can help combat test anxiety.

When you nurture your physical health, you are also contributing to your mental health. If your body is healthy, your mind is much more likely to be healthy as well. So take time to rest, nourish your body with healthy food and water, and get moving as much as possible. Taking these physical steps will make you stronger and more able to take the mental steps necessary to overcome test anxiety.

Mental Steps for Beating Test Anxiety

Working on the mental side of test anxiety can be more challenging, but as with the physical side, there are clear steps you can take to overcome it. As mentioned earlier, test anxiety often stems from lack of preparation, so the obvious solution is to prepare for the test. Effective studying may be the most important weapon you have for beating test anxiety, but you can and should employ several other mental tools to combat fear.

First, boost your confidence by reminding yourself of past success—tests or projects that you aced. If you're putting as much effort into preparing for this test as you did for those, there's no reason you should expect to fail here. Work hard to prepare; then trust your preparation.

Second, surround yourself with encouraging people. It can be helpful to find a study group, but be sure that the people you're around will encourage a positive attitude. If you spend time with others who are anxious or cynical, this will only contribute to your own anxiety. Look for others who are motivated to study hard from a desire to succeed, not from a fear of failure.

Third, reward yourself. A test is physically and mentally tiring, even without anxiety, and it can be helpful to have something to look forward to. Plan an activity following the test, regardless of the outcome, such as going to a movie or getting ice cream.

When you are taking the test, if you find yourself beginning to feel anxious, remind yourself that you know the material. Visualize successfully completing the test. Then take a few deep, relaxing breaths and return to it. Work through the questions carefully but with confidence, knowing that you are capable of succeeding.

Developing a healthy mental approach to test taking will also aid in other areas of life. Test anxiety affects more than just the actual test—it can be damaging to your mental health and even contribute to depression. It's important to beat test anxiety before it becomes a problem for more than testing.

Study Strategy

Being prepared for the test is necessary to combat anxiety, but what does being prepared look like? You may study for hours on end and still not feel prepared. What you need is a strategy for test prep. The next few pages outline our recommended steps to help you plan out and conquer the challenge of preparation.

Step 1: Scope Out the Test

Learn everything you can about the format (multiple choice, essay, etc.) and what will be on the test. Gather any study materials, course outlines, or sample exams that may be available. Not only will this help you to prepare, but knowing what to expect can help to alleviate test anxiety.

Step 2: Map Out the Material

Look through the textbook or study guide and make note of how many chapters or sections it has. Then divide these over the time you have. For example, if a book has 15 chapters and you have five days to study, you need to cover three chapters each day. Even better, if you have the time, leave an extra day at the end for overall review after you have gone through the material in depth.

If time is limited, you may need to prioritize the material. Look through it and make note of which sections you think you already have a good grasp on, and which need review. While you are studying, skim quickly through the familiar sections and take more time on the challenging parts.

Write out your plan so you don't get lost as you go. Having a written plan also helps you feel more in control of the study, so anxiety is less likely to arise from feeling overwhelmed at the amount to cover.

STEP 3: GATHER YOUR TOOLS

Decide what study method works best for you. Do you prefer to highlight in the book as you study and then go back over the highlighted portions? Or do you type out notes of the important information? Or is it helpful to make flashcards that you can carry with you? Assemble the pens, index cards, highlighters, post-it notes, and any other materials you may need so you won't be distracted by getting up to find things while you study.

If you're having a hard time retaining the information or organizing your notes, experiment with different methods. For example, try color-coding by subject with colored pens, highlighters, or post-it notes. If you learn better by hearing, try recording yourself reading your notes so you can listen while in the car, working out, or simply sitting at your desk. Ask a friend to quiz you from your flashcards, or try teaching someone the material to solidify it in your mind.

STEP 4: CREATE YOUR ENVIRONMENT

It's important to avoid distractions while you study. This includes both the obvious distractions like visitors and the subtle distractions like an uncomfortable chair (or a too-comfortable couch that makes you want to fall asleep). Set up the best study environment possible: good lighting and a comfortable work area. If background music helps you focus, you may want to turn it on, but otherwise keep the room quiet. If you are using a computer to take notes, be sure you don't have any other windows open, especially applications like social media, games, or anything else that could distract you. Silence your phone and turn off notifications. Be sure to keep water close by so you stay hydrated while you study (but avoid unhealthy drinks and snacks).

Also, take into account the best time of day to study. Are you freshest first thing in the morning? Try to set aside some time then to work through the material. Is your mind clearer in the afternoon or evening? Schedule your study session then. Another method is to study at the same time of day that you will take the test, so that your brain gets used to working on the material at that time and will be ready to focus at test time.

STEP 5: STUDY!

Once you have done all the study preparation, it's time to settle into the actual studying. Sit down, take a few moments to settle your mind so you can focus, and begin to follow your study plan. Don't give in to distractions or let yourself procrastinate. This is your time to prepare so you'll be ready to fearlessly approach the test. Make the most of the time and stay focused.

Of course, you don't want to burn out. If you study too long you may find that you're not retaining the information very well. Take regular study breaks. For example, taking five minutes out of every hour to walk briskly, breathing deeply and swinging your arms, can help your mind stay fresh.

As you get to the end of each chapter or section, it's a good idea to do a quick review. Remind yourself of what you learned and work on any difficult parts. When you feel that you've mastered the material, move on to the next part. At the end of your study session, briefly skim through your notes again.

But while review is helpful, cramming last minute is NOT. If at all possible, work ahead so that you won't need to fit all your study into the last day. Cramming overloads your brain with more information than it can process and retain, and your tired mind may struggle to recall even previously learned information when it is overwhelmed with last-minute study. Also, the urgent nature of cramming and the stress placed on your brain contribute to anxiety. You'll be more likely to go to the test feeling unprepared and having trouble thinking clearly.

So don't cram, and don't stay up late before the test, even just to review your notes at a leisurely pace. Your brain needs rest more than it needs to go over the information again. In fact, plan to finish your studies by noon or early afternoon the day before the test. Give your brain the rest of the day to relax or focus on other things, and get a good night's sleep. Then you will be fresh for the test and better able to recall what you've studied.

Step 6: Take a Practice Test

Many courses offer sample tests, either online or in the study materials. This is an excellent resource to check whether you have mastered the material, as well as to prepare for the test format and environment.

Check the test format ahead of time: the number of questions, the type (multiple choice, free response, etc.), and the time limit. Then create a plan for working through them. For example, if you have 30 minutes to take a 60-question test, your limit is 30 seconds per question. Spend less time on the questions you know well so that you can take more time on the difficult ones.

If you have time to take several practice tests, take the first one open book, with no time limit. Work through the questions at your own pace and make sure you fully understand them. Gradually work up to taking a test under test conditions: sit at a desk with all study materials put away and set a timer. Pace yourself to make sure you finish the test with time to spare and go back to check your answers if you have time.

After each test, check your answers. On the questions you missed, be sure you understand why you missed them. Did you misread the question (tests can use tricky wording)? Did you forget the information? Or was it something you hadn't learned? Go back and study any shaky areas that the practice tests reveal.

Taking these tests not only helps with your grade, but also aids in combating test anxiety. If you're already used to the test conditions, you're less likely to worry about it, and working through tests until you're scoring well gives you a confidence boost. Go through the practice tests until you feel comfortable, and then you can go into the test knowing that you're ready for it.

Test Tips

On test day, you should be confident, knowing that you've prepared well and are ready to answer the questions. But aside from preparation, there are several test day strategies you can employ to maximize your performance.

First, as stated before, get a good night's sleep the night before the test (and for several nights before that, if possible). Go into the test with a fresh, alert mind rather than staying up late to study.

Try not to change too much about your normal routine on the day of the test. It's important to eat a nutritious breakfast, but if you normally don't eat breakfast at all, consider eating just a protein bar. If you're a coffee drinker, go ahead and have your normal coffee. Just make sure you time it so that the caffeine doesn't wear off right in the middle of your test. Avoid sugary beverages, and drink enough water to stay hydrated but not so much that you need a restroom break 10 minutes into the test. If your test isn't first thing in the morning, consider going for a walk or doing a light workout before the test to get your blood flowing.

Allow yourself enough time to get ready, and leave for the test with plenty of time to spare so you won't have the anxiety of scrambling to arrive in time. Another reason to be early is to select a good seat. It's helpful to sit away from doors and windows, which can be distracting. Find a good seat, get out your supplies, and settle your mind before the test begins.

When the test begins, start by going over the instructions carefully, even if you already know what to expect. Make sure you avoid any careless mistakes by following the directions.

Then begin working through the questions, pacing yourself as you've practiced. If you're not sure on an answer, don't spend too much time on it, and don't let it shake your confidence. Either skip it and come back later, or eliminate as many wrong answers as possible and guess among the remaining ones. Don't dwell on these questions as you continue—put them out of your mind and focus on what lies ahead.

Be sure to read all of the answer choices, even if you're sure the first one is the right answer. Sometimes you'll find a better one if you keep reading. But don't second-guess yourself if you do immediately know the answer. Your gut instinct is usually right. Don't let test anxiety rob you of the information you know.

If you have time at the end of the test (and if the test format allows), go back and review your answers. Be cautious about changing any, since your first instinct tends to be correct, but make sure you didn't misread any of the questions or accidentally mark the wrong answer choice. Look over any you skipped and make an educated guess.

At the end, leave the test feeling confident. You've done your best, so don't waste time worrying about your performance or wishing you could change anything. Instead, celebrate the successful completion of this test. And finally, use this test to learn how to deal with anxiety even better next time.

Review Video: Test Anxiety
Visit mometrix.com/academy and enter code: 100340

Important Qualification

Not all anxiety is created equal. If your test anxiety is causing major issues in your life beyond the classroom or testing center, or if you are experiencing troubling physical symptoms related to your anxiety, it may be a sign of a serious physiological or psychological condition. If this sounds like your situation, we strongly encourage you to seek professional help.

Thank You

We at Mometrix would like to extend our heartfelt thanks to you, our friend and patron, for allowing us to play a part in your journey. It is a privilege to serve people from all walks of life who are unified in their commitment to building the best future they can for themselves.

The preparation you devote to these important testing milestones may be the most valuable educational opportunity you have for making a real difference in your life. We encourage you to put your heart into it—that feeling of succeeding, overcoming, and yes, conquering will be well worth the hours you've invested.

We want to hear your story, your struggles and your successes, and if you see any opportunities for us to improve our materials so we can help others even more effectively in the future, please share that with us as well. **The team at Mometrix would be absolutely thrilled to hear from you!** So please, send us an email (support@mometrix.com) and let's stay in touch.

If you'd like some additional help, check out these other resources we offer for your exam:
http://MometrixFlashcards.com/SOL

Online Resources

Due to our efforts to try to keep this book to a manageable length, we've created a link that will give you access to all of your online resources:

mometrix.com/resources719/vsolwhist1

It's Your Moment, Let's Celebrate It!

Share your story @mometrixtestpreparation